Health Essentials

Spiritual Healing

Jack Angelo studied Education and Art at London University. He taught slow learning and emotionally disturbed children in London for eleven years before moving to Wales to pursue studies in subtle energy and healing. Dr Angelo is a national tutor for the National Federation of Spiritual Healers. He writes and runs courses on subtle energy healing, both in the UK and abroad. He has been awarded an honorary doctorate for his work in the field.

The Health Essentials Series

There is a growing number of people who find themselves attracted to holistic or alternative therapies and natural approaches to maintaining optimum health and vitality. The *Health Essentials* series is designed to help the newcomer by presenting high quality introductions to all the main complementary health subjects. Each book presents all the essential information on each therapy, explaining what it is, how it works and what it can do for the reader. Advice is also given, where possible, on how to begin using the therapy at home, together with comprehensive lists of courses and classes available worldwide.

The *Health Essentials* titles are all written by practising experts in their fields. Exceptionally clear and concise, each text is supported by attractive illustrations.

Series Medical Consultant
Dr John Cosh MD, FRCP

In the same series

Acupressure by Richard Brennan
Acupuncture by Peter Mole
Alexander Technique by Richard Brennan
Aromatherapy by Christine Wildwood
Ayurveda by Scott Gerson
Chi Kung by James MacRitchie
Chinese Medicine by Tom Williams
Colour Therapy by Pauline Wills
Flower Remedies by Christine Wildwood
Herbal Medicine by Vicki Pitman
Homeopathy by Peter Adams
Iridology by John and Sheelagh Colton
Kinesiology by Ann Holdway
Massage by Stewart Mitchell
Natural Beauty by Sidra Shaukat
Reflexology by Inge Dougans with Suzanne Ellis
Self-Hypnosis by Elaine Sheehan
Shiatsu by Elaine Liechti
Vitamin Guide by Hasnain Walji

Health Essentials

SPIRITUAL HEALING

Energy Medicine for Health and Wellbeing

JACK ANGELO

ELEMENT

Shaftesbury, Dorset ● Boston, Massachusetts
Melbourne, Victoria

First published in Great Britain in 1991 by
Element Books Limited
Shaftesbury, Dorset SP7 8BP

Published in the USA in 1991 by
Element Books, Inc.
160 North Washington Street
Boston, MA 02114

Published in Australia in 1994 by
Element Books and distributed by
Penguin Australia Limited
487 Maroondah Highway
Ringwood, Victoria 3134

Reprinted 1995

Reissued 1998

Cover design by Slatter-Anderson
Design by Roger Lightfoot

Typeset by Palimpsest Book Production Limited,
Polmont, Stirlingshire
Printed and bound in Great Britain by
Biddles Ltd, Guildford and Kings Lynn

British Library Cataloguing in Publication
data available

Library of Congress Cataloging in Publication
data
Angelo, Jack.
Spiritual healing / Jack Angelo.
p.   cm. – – (Health essentials series)
Includes bibliographical references and index.
ISBN 1-85230-219-4 (pb): $9.95
1. Mental healing. 2. Spiritual healing. I. Title.   II. Series.
RZ401.A66 1991
615.8'52 – –dc20   91-36713 CIP

ISBN 1–85230–219–4

Note from the Publisher

Any information given in any book in the *Health Essentials*
series is not intended to be taken as a replacement for medical
advice. Any person with a condition requiring medical attention should consult a qualified medical practitioner or suitable
therapist.

Contents

1. What is Spiritual Healing?   1
2. What Spiritual Healing Can Do for You   17
3. The Human Energy Field   42
4. What It Means to be a Healer   63
5. The Range of Healing   74
6. Healing and the Cycle of Life   88
7. Taking It Further   104
Notes and References   117
Further Reading   118
Glossary   119
Index   121

Acknowledgements

I WOULD LIKE to thank my wife Jan for her constant support and inspiration during all stages of the book.

Many patients and healers have been consulted regarding the casework and I thank them all for their help. Names and situations have been changed to protect their privacy.

Note to the Reader

The masculine pronoun has been used throughout this book as a convention. It is intended to imply both male and female genders where this is applicable.

When we link, with love, to the light that is everywhere – healing must follow.

1

What is Spiritual Healing?

WHEN WE FEEL a pain we put our hands over the place that hurts, just as a mother does when her child is in distress. The wish to help another in this way is a desire which comes from the heart and the action involves the hands. This timeless gesture is as old as mankind, as old, as necessary and as natural as stroking, caressing, hugging or embracing.

The evidence that it is a healing gesture goes back thousands of years to the friezes of Egyptian tombs and temples, to the ancient healing practices of the Kahunas of Polynesia and the Aboriginal peoples of Australasia and America. In Sanskrit, Chinese and Aramaic texts, the laying on of hands was paramount in all healing activity. Very often this took place in conjunction with the use of herbs, bleeding, baths, medicines, potions and ointments. It was even extended to include such techniques as massage, manipulation, shiatsu or reflexology.

We have all felt the reassurance, warmth or comfort of another's touch. We have also felt the antagonistic or rejecting touch. There is more, then, to the healing touch than mere gesture. Something is transmitted from one person to another. The healing touch, whether on or near the body, transmits positive energies which can, and do, heal.

The effects of such energies are not only to heal bodies but minds and emotions too. Spiritual healing is the channelling of healing energy from its spiritual source to the one who is in need of help. Sometimes the channel for this energy is a healer and perhaps the most common method of transference is through the hands. All healers train to be as pure a channel as possible so that the patient will receive the maximum benefit according to his needs.

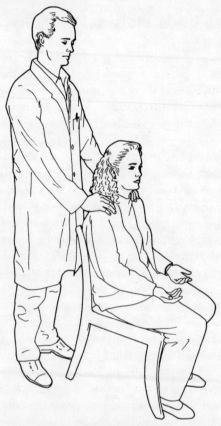

Fig. 1. *Patient and healer*

To understand what spiritual healing is and how it works we need to understand ourselves and the state of existence in which we find ourselves. This will lead to a better understanding of health and ill health so that we may use this knowledge to enhance our lives and bring into focus our reasons for being here. We all have a reason for being here and our health or ill health is intimately linked with our own personal quest. The spirit within, our higher self, knows what this quest is and how it can be achieved here on Earth.

HUMANS AS SPIRITUAL BEINGS

We are spiritual beings living in a spiritual universe where matter vibrates at different speeds. This creates the different levels of existence. On every level spirit needs a vehicle which is compatible with its surroundings, that is, which vibrates at the same rate. On the physical level our vehicle is the physical body.

What needs to be remembered is that we, as spirit beings, are bathed, as it were, in the universal energy field of the spiritual universe. All vibrations of matter surround us, not just the physical, so that we experience more than one level of existence at the same time. This is occurring even though we are not conscious of it just as, when in the bath, we may only be conscious of the telephone ringing rather than the scent of the bath oil or the feeling of the sponge nestling against our toes. The extent of our consciousness depends on how much information we can handle at any one time and, for most of us, consciousness of just one thing at a time is quite enough!

Thus it becomes quickly apparent that, if we think of existence in terms of the physical level alone, in spite of the evidence to the contrary, the real truth about ourselves will remain hidden and our view of life severely limited. In the same way, this view will also obscure the real truth about our well-being. We need to realize that, more often than not, any form of ill health is an alarm bell, our way of alerting ourselves to the fact that there is also some disharmony on one or more of the other levels of our being.

The energies of a healthy person are totally balanced. It is our higher self which is capable of regulating and balancing these energies to bring about harmony. So it is with the patient's higher self that the spiritual healer works since this

3

is the human facet which is able to assess and monitor all levels at the same time.

Spiritual healing complements orthodox medicine, which attends to our physical needs, by extending therapy to the other levels of our essential nature, to discover what may be the underlying cause of the condition.

A Fourfold Vision

In an attempt to explain these other aspects of our life, mystics and psychologists of all schools have given us a list of terms which at first sight appears very confusing. This book uses *spirit* to mean the complete spiritual being; *higher self* to mean the aspect of spirit which is directly linked to the spiritual source of all that is; *mind*, the mental instrument of spirit; *emotions*, the feeling aspect of spirit; *body*, the physical vehicle of spirit.

The human spirit is on a journey of experience and evolution from its original spiritual source, via encounters on all levels of existence, back to the source of all that is – the source of all energy. A record of our experiences and insights is kept in the subconscious mind. As explained earlier, because there are many levels of existence, human experience is multi-dimensional though we are hardly ever aware of this simultaneously. For example, we are aware of physical life but we are only aware of a dream existence in the sleep state. As we create pictures in our imagination or fantasize, we tend to become less aware of everyday physical sensations.

For the purposes of this book, the vision of ourselves is fourfold – spirit having at least four aspects of being through which it is expressing itself. The aspect having a direct connection with the spiritual source is our higher self or soul. Some authorities call this aspect of spirit the 'true' self which is perhaps unfortunate since it implies that all other aspects of self are false. This is a philosophical point and to argue for, or against, will not help our understanding of spiritual healing.

The second aspect of spirit is mind. Through it we can be conscious of mental levels of existence. The third aspect is the emotions and through them we can be conscious of

4

emotional or feeling levels of existence. Finally, the physical aspect which is the material vehicle that spirit uses to exist on the physical level of Earth.

This division of spirit (which is not, in reality, divided but whole) is made simply to talk about the different levels of our being with which all healers have to deal. All the four aspects are interrelated and interconnected and go to make the wonderful entities that we are. Because of their interrelation healers must be aware of them all.

Understanding the Causes of Ill Health

The role of the mind and the emotions in creating disease or harmony is now accepted. We talk of mental and emotional health as well as physical health. But these are aspects of spirit and it is the lack of understanding of this unifying truth which has so far been the missing piece in the jigsaw of human health for both layman and physician. Once doctors acknowledge this and begin to work with healers, as many now do, the patient immediately benefits. Another function of spiritual healing, then, is to create awareness in the medical profession and the general public of our spiritual nature and to bring this awareness into focus – to the benefit of all concerned.

Spiritual healing awakens us to the presence of the higher self, what the healer Harry Edwards called 'the latent divinity within'. Furthermore, it demonstrates that being cut off from our higher self may be one of the causes of ill health or the cause of our misunderstanding of ill health. It demonstrates that spirit is not opposed to body, nor body to spirit, for the two are aspects of the same. Rather, awareness of our spirituality transcends all separations and barriers, bringing a state of connectedness to the Source, other people and the world around us. It defines our relationship with the universe and with the infinite of which it is a part. It confirms and uses our capacity to be energized from beyond ourselves. As beings of energy we are dynamic, in motion, reaching out to touch and interact with all other energies.

Allowing ourselves to be touched and to interact with the

energies of healing will bring about a realignment in our own
energy systems. This is a challenge to operate as complete
people, a challenge to be truly ourselves. So ill health may
be seen from a positive point of view as our body's way of
presenting this challenge.

HISTORICAL PERSPECTIVE

Since the middle of this century, thanks to the pioneering
work of healers like Harry Edwards, the number of practitioners
around the world has grown to many thousands and their
healing organizations are now government-recognized. With
the General Medical Council of the UK allowing doctors to
recommend spiritual healing to their patients, both in general
practice and in hospitals, this gentle and benign therapy has
come a long way. The healing organizations are justly proud
of this progress for, in the past, spiritual healing has had to
struggle against ignorance, fear and persecution.

Healing in Biblical Times

At the time of Pythagoras (sixth century BC) healing was
an integral part of therapeutic practice, along with many
other forms of 'alternative medicine'. It was well known
that some healers possessed greater powers than others and
that many of these came from communities where healers
could undergo special training. Typical of such groups were
the Essenes.

This desert brotherhood lived by the shores of the Dead
Sea in Palestine and at Lake Mareotis in Egypt. They lived
a life in tune with both the cosmos and nature, close to what
they called their 'Earthly Mother'. They studied Chaldean and
Persian astronomy and were adept in the arts of healing. Essene
healers had to undergo a year's probation and three years of
initiatory work before they were allowed access to the more
advanced teachings.

The Essenes' proficiency as healers was well known in Asia

and the Middle East. The Greeks called them the Therapeutae because of the quality of their counselling and patient care. From this background came the prophet Elijah, John the Baptist, John the Beloved and the great Essene Master Jesus.

Jesus once assured his followers that healers would come after him who would do 'even greater works' than he. In spite of his words, as the Christian Church became institutionalized, the widespread practice of laying on of hands began to be more and more restricted to ordained ministers of religion. This movement away from the layman with the gift of healing not only met with official approval but came to be rigorously enforced.

It had long been noted by the Church that healers, just as they are described in the Old Testament, possessed other abilities such as clairvoyance and clairaudience. These are abilities of high sense perception by which a human being may see or hear higher vibrations than those usually sensed. The Book of Kings, for example, describes the range of gifts possessed by the prophets Elisha and Elijah (1 Kings 17, 2 Kings 4, 2 Kings 5). Apart from healing, they could also predict future events, multiply food and recover lost items by psychic means.

The Effects of Persecution

Church policy ruled that such abilities linked healers to the old pagan religions rather than the great prophets. From Anglo-Saxon times spiritually gifted people had been called witches from the root word *wit* meaning 'wise person'. But it became official policy to take every step to ensure that the word 'witch' was equated with evil rather than wisdom in the public mind. This campaign allowed the Inquisition and, later, the Protestant Church, brutally to punish healers or even put them to death.

The Churches had no monopoly on persecution. In earlier times, the Book of Samuel, for example, tells how King Saul 'put away' all psychically gifted people including healers. Yet he still went secretly to see a woman medium in the hope of

7

getting a message from the 'dead' Samuel on how to defeat the Philistines (1 Samuel 28).

This account appears in the Authorized Version of the Bible but, at the time of its publication in 1611, persons with such gifts were said to be in league with the Devil. Hence, the gentle and compassionate woman mentioned in the text was known as 'the witch of Endor'.

By the time the King James Bible found a place on British lecterns, some 300,000 psychics and healers had been executed over the course of 200 years and Parliament's Statute of Persecution continued to permit executions until its repeal in 1735. Since the persecutions were, in effect, a denial of the source of all healing energy it is hardly surprising that the power of ministers of the Church to heal diminished at the same time.

This rapid decline in the number of people who could care for those suffering from ill health opened the way for a new class of healers. These were the physicians who, from the time of Hippocrates (fourth century BC), had been developing a form of medicine based on physical criteria alone. They were the forerunners of the doctors and surgeons of today. This development in therapeutic practice marked the shift away from a holistic approach to health for it favoured a regime which treated the condition rather than the patient, the symptoms rather than the cause of disease.

Healers and psychics had acted as a living bridge between the spiritual and the temporal but, with this group virtually eradicated, human life could more easily become fragmented. From the Middle Ages onwards the rift widened between things material – the here and now – and things spiritual, the hereafter. Medicine, no longer having a close link with spiritual teachings, became progressively allied with a physical view of the body alone. Finally, with the acceptance of Newtonian science and a mechanistic world-view, the Age of Reason (eighteenth century) saw ill health as a breakdown in the human machine which should be reparable by scientific means.

Modern Developments

The Age of Aquarius was still a century away yet the effects of its coming were already beginning to be felt. From the eighteenth century, people sought freedom in all aspects of life, especially religion, and healing was already being revived in the new chapels and religious communities of Europe and America. By the middle of the nineteenth century various movements sought to narrow the gap between scientific medicine and spiritual healing by demonstrating the link between the spiritual source of healing energy and its effects on the physical body. The most well known, though perhaps the most confused in its teachings, was the Church of Christ, Scientist, founded in America by Mary Baker Eddy in 1866. Such movements symbolized the growing need for a spiritual dimension to human life and health care which both the Church and medicine seemed to be failing to provide.

In the nineteenth century the USA was also the birthplace of startling new developments, the repercussions of which will be felt into the twenty-first century. These were the attempts by entities on higher frequencies of existence (sometimes called 'the spirit world') to make contact with people here on the physical level of Earth. They informed American psychics that the human race was ready for a new and powerful input of spiritual energy. This would affect all aspects of our being, reawaken healing and other subtle energies in people and so change the course of human history.

The loving entities who brought this dramatic message said they were spirit, just like us. The only difference between us and them was that they had no need of a physical body but, being human, they still wanted to make all the resources of spirit available to human beings on Earth in the next crucial stage of their progress. They also explained that communication with entities such as themselves would increase rapidly in the coming 150 years and play a vital role in the re-establishment of contact with universal forces.

Just as the visiting entities had prophesied, various 'gifts of the spirit' soon manifested in people all over the world,

9

especially women. Because of the legal statutes of the time, many thought it prudent to incorporate these spiritual gifts into a religious framework and so the Spiritualist religion was born – also known as Spiritism in South America.

DEVELOPMENT OF SPIRITUAL HEALING

Perhaps the greatest spiritual gift which was returned to us was the gift of healing. This was still allowed within the context of the established Church, even though it was not widely practised, but legally denied to those who might wish to practise, or avail themselves of it, outside. Further legal constraints forced spiritual healing to remain within the Spiritualist movement so that many people still think that they are synonymous. In 1938, for example, the Cancer Act made it an offence in the UK for any spiritual healer to lay hands on a sufferer. It was also an indictable offence for a healer to treat cancer by distant healing.

By then spiritual healing was being practised in every Spiritualist church and by numerous healers working outside it. In 1946, when Harry Edwards wrote *Psychic Healing* (later retitled *Spirit Healing*) he had already given healing to thousands of people all over Britain, both privately and at massive public-healing demonstrations, yet this foremost gift of the spirit was only made legal in the UK five years later. This was largely due to the public pressure built up by the work of healers throughout the country, the growing reputation of Harry Edwards' Healing Sanctuary and the support from eminent persons of the day who had witnessed the beneficial effects of spiritual healing. For example, Sir William Barrett, FRS, who was Professor of Physics at the Royal College of Science, echoed the words of St Augustine when he said that healing miracles did not happen in contradiction to nature, nor were they supernatural events – it was simply that they transcended what was presently known of natural forces.

Like many scientists, Sir William understood the effect on science of its centuries-old separation from spiritual levels of knowledge. This divorce had obliged all branches of scientific endeavour to be materially based, depriving them of the chance to integrate their findings with those working on other levels.

Of all scientists, perhaps physicists have found this restriction the most intolerable since their researches have taken them to the point where neither religion nor other disciplines can provide answers to their questions. Modern medicine finds itself in the same predicament, having had to move away from a biomedical model, firmly grounded in the mechanistic approach to the human body, in order to acknowledge the role of the mind and the emotions in pathology.

Understandably, in view of its history and evolution, medical practice still finds no role for the spirit. Illness may be 'psychosomatic', there may be 'spontaneous remissions' or just plain incorrect diagnoses, but if there is an explanation outside current medical experience it is because the relevant research has not yet been done.

Spiritual healers would agree that research is vital and welcome it. If a technique is to attain credibility there must be evidence to support it. But they would also agree with physicist Fritjof Capra[1] that the scientific method is to base a hypothesis on the collection of data. The records of healers around the world, concerning hundreds of thousands of patients, are data which it would be unscientific to ignore. Perhaps they are difficult to understand but, as Sir William Barrett once pointed out, this is due to the level of our investigations and the state of our knowledge. Hindsight shows that this situation is only temporary and that one day we will understand.

When healing became the responsibility of physicians, the patient's personal responsibility for his own well-being was effectively transferred. Spiritual healing helps a patient to see the truth about himself and his condition. It goes beyond the symptoms to treat and heal the cause of the physical, mental, emotional or spiritual problem. In doing so, the patient is given back control over his own health and his own destiny.

But this is not necessarily what a patient may be asking of a healer. He may seek something quite basic, such as the cessation of pain. And why not? The healer is there to serve and the relief of suffering is the first aim. That other levels will be touched during a healing session is certain, however, and the patient can only benefit from this.

SOME FIRST CONTACTS WITH HEALING

A person's first contact with spiritual healing may be at one of the health or complementary therapy exhibitions held in cities and towns. This allows the visitor to see what goes on during a healing session and perhaps to sample it himself. The National Federation of Spiritual Healers runs a 'Healing Garden' at most of these events and has an active policy of reaching out to the public to allow them to dip into healing in whatever way they wish. Healers are always on hand to talk to people and explain what is happening.

A second way of seeing healing in progress is at a public-healing demonstration. This is usually an event devoted entirely to healing where, again, people may watch and participate if they feel the need.

Some healers work privately, in healing centres and clinics, or both. Referral lists of registered healers are kept by the organizations mentioned in Chapter 7 which can inform the patient of the location of their nearest healer.

After having made the appointment it is a good plan to go with a friend or relative. They will be allowed to be present during the healing session. This is especially necessary where emotional support may be needed. Most healers prefer a patient of the opposite sex to be accompanied, for obvious ethical reasons.

Healers belonging to registered organizations also visit patients in hospitals and hospices. At all times it is the hospital which is in charge and a healer will only work there with the full agreement of both patient and hospital staff. There are now many hospitals and hospices which are happy to allow healers into their wards and are pleased with the raising of morale and relief from pain which healing brings.

THE CODE OF CONDUCT

Patients thinking about visiting a healer should realize that all registered healers adhere to a strict code of conduct. This Code has been drawn up by the Confederation of Healing Organisations in consultation with the BMA, the General Medical Council and the Royal Colleges of Surgeons, General Practitioners, Midwives, and Nursing. The following principles are extracted from the Code:

* Healing must only be given in response to an invitation from the patient or his representative.
* Healers must treat as confidential all information of a personal nature which is confided by the patient.
* Recovery must never be promised and healers must never undermine the patient's faith in hospital treatment or regime.
* Healers must not countermand instructions or prescriptions given by a doctor nor must they give a medical diagnosis to a patient in any circumstances.
* Healers are advised not to give healing to a child under the age of sixteen unless medical aid has first been sought by a parent or guardian.
* Healers are not allowed by law to practise dentistry nor to attend women in childbirth or within ten days thereafter.
* Healers may give healing to people with AIDS but it is illegal to treat anyone suffering from a venereal disease unless this service is entirely free.
* Healing of animals by the laying on of hands, by distant healing or prayer, is legal and acceptable to the Royal College of Veterinary Surgeons.

The Healing Session

When seeing a spiritual healer the patient can first of all expect to be put at ease. He will not be asked to take off any clothing except a coat and footwear, but he will be asked to make himself comfortable. The healer will ask about his condition, whether he has consulted a doctor, and anything else which seems relevant to the case. The patient can be confident that the healer will take the time to listen to his replies and may be surprised that most healers are prepared to spend a good deal of time at this stage – the initial consultation.

The healer may take notes or make a tape recording of the interview for his own records or to enable him to return to important points at a later stage in the treatment. Such records remain completely confidential. The interview, the sympathetic listening and any counselling are all part of the treatment which begins, in the case of spiritual healing, as soon as a person asks for help.

The patient may need to be shown how to sit or lie down correctly and the healer helps him to relax mentally and physically and to leave any stress outside the treatment room or healing sanctuary.

Some patients find the physical contact of the healer's hands comforting and reassuring, but most healers prefer to keep their hands at a short distance from the patient's body. This latter procedure will always be the case where delicate areas, genital areas or the breasts of a woman are concerned. It is also the method used to 'scan' the patient and to assess the level of balance in his energy systems.

If he has not already sought attunement with the patient's higher self, the healer will do so now. Soon after this, patients may sense the flow of energy in their own bodies as feelings of warmth, cooling, tingling or light-headedness, generally accompanied by feelings of relaxation and letting go. Once he allows the healing energies to interact with his own system, the patient's needs will dictate the course of the treatment. They will determine, for example, how long each treatment lasts, how often and at what intervals he may need further treatments.

Immediately following a treatment a patient may feel very thirsty. If so he will be encouraged to drink as much plain water as he wishes. Conversely, he may need to visit the toilet and should do so! A feeling of drowsiness is common and, noting this, the healer will advise a patient not to drive until this feeling wears off. This is another good reason for going with a friend.

Usually there needs to be a gap between sessions to give the treatment time to work on as many levels as possible. The healer will advise whether and when another session is necessary and will keep to this unless some sort of emergency occurs.

The patient should keep a careful note of any change in his condition, even of any significant dreams or new thought patterns. These events will be part of the feedback which is so essential in strengthening the link between patient, healer and spirit. The healer will be pleased to answer any queries which arise out of the feedback or the treatment and to show whether they may be part of the patient's progress. A patient may rest assured that healers cooperate with doctors and would be delighted to work more closely with them if the doctor saw fit.

IS FAITH NECESSARY?

People often think that spiritual healing is faith healing and there is no doubt that faith, or a positive attitude towards healing, will help tremendously because this enables the patient to be fully open to the flow of energy. The term 'spiritual' refers to the source of healing energy, a spiritual one. How this high frequency energy is stepped down through the medium of a healer will be discussed in detail in Chapter 3.

Apart from the benefit mentioned, there is no need for patients to have any religious faith and, as long as they are open to healing, their own religious faith or otherwise will not affect the outcome. Neither small children nor animals could be said to have faith yet healing is just as effective in their case.

The healer will assume that the patient has the will to get better and this is why he is seeking help. This attitude can be further reinforced by thinking positively and creatively about restoring bodily health and peace of mind and by interacting positively and kindly with others. Where the will needs strengthening or a negative attitude needs changing, healing will be directed to these levels also.

Spending a few moments each day to relax and attune with the spirit within, just as in the healing session, will build and maintain the balance and harmony that is needed.

By fully cooperating with the healer, the patient is cooperating with his higher self and taking responsibility for his own health. In doing so he becomes an active participant in the art and science of spiritual healing. This is a therapeutic process which restores health and vitality to all levels of our being, no matter where ill health may be manifesting.

2

What Spiritual Healing Can Do for You

CREATING THE HEALING ENERGY PATTERN

HEALING ACTUALLY STARTS with the call for help, either by the patient or someone acting on his behalf. The call may be by telephone, letter or personal visit to a healer. This makes a temporary link with the healer that allows him to be a channel through which healing energies can begin to flow. Even thinking about a healer in this context will create the necessary link.

On receiving the call the healer attunes his thoughts to the life force itself and those who are able to direct it. He then attunes himself to the patient, which effectively reawakens the patient's own link with the Source of healing. We are always connected to the Source through our higher self, but in times of trouble or ill health it may seem impossible to realise this and allow healing to flow directly to us. By contacting a healer we start to create the conditions for this flow to take place (see Fig. 2.).

Many healers describe how they have said 'yes' to a patient's telephone call and then forgotten all about it. The same day the patient calls again to say he is feeling much better. This demonstrates how the triangle of healing is always available for any patient or healer to tap into. The mind makes the link and the energy structure provides the means whereby healing can immediately begin its work.

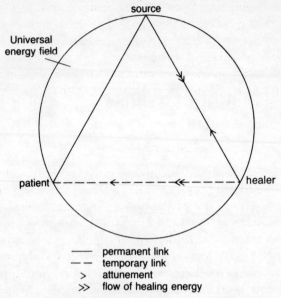

Fig. 2. The healing triangle: energy links and flow between patient, healer and the Source of healing energies

As it flows into the patient's system it is accepted at a spiritual level, opening up the connection with the spirit and putting the patient back in touch with life. The healing force moves into, and touches, every level of being to set in motion the body's natural healing processes. It can change the very atomic structure of the human body, reprogramme negative thinking and heal the effects of destructive emotions. In this way healing transforms conditions and changes lives through the transmission of appropriate energies.

This chapter gives an overview of what these energies can do. There are no limits to the range of health problems which healing can deal with – from a cut or bruise to the most life-threatening conditions such as cancer or AIDS. Spiritual healing has something to give to any problem concerning any aspect of a person's life. Healers deal with emotional and mental problems as much as physical ones and many are expert counsellors, family and social therapists.

18

The only limits are those which a healer may impose on his work, such as specializing in certain conditions, or those which the patient imposes. There are many causes of ill health, some of which may be bound up with a person's reason for coming to Earth. Various limitations which a patient could impose on treatment are explained in the context of the case histories which follow.

Levels of Healing

It is true to say that because healing energies originate at a spiritual level they can work on any facet of a person's being. Sometimes the physical body is the last level to be influenced because the condition has been created by problems on subtler levels. The healer will be able to warn the patient if this is the case so that he can look out for changes in, say, attitudes or outlook, which will assure him that the treatment is 'working'. Some healers deal with a patient's problem in a very simple way. Others offer counselling and an explanation of their actions if the patient asks for this or if the healer senses that it will help. No two healers work the same way and patients should always feel free to find a healer with whom they feel comfortable. This is where personal recommendation can often be of help.

Healers are ordinary people, like their patients, which means that they, too, are at different levels of personal development. This has a lot to do with how a healer works, whether he specializes in certain complaints or accepts whatever comes his way. It also determines whether a healer is prepared to involve himself in the whole range of life's circumstances where healing may have a positive effect.

Ways of Working with Healing Energies

When the healer attunes himself to become a channel for healing energies, his mind reaches levels beyond the physical. It must do so for this is where healing energies originate. Once the healer's being is attuned in this way, it allows three basic processes to take place:

1. If he is receptive to healing power and able to use it consciously himself, he will do this.
2. He may have the ability to allow entities on other levels to direct and assist him in how to use healing power.
3. He may have the capacity to allow these entities to use his own energy systems to manifest their healing abilities through him.

In the first process the healer is able to realize what energies are needed to deal with a specific condition. He knows how to draw them in from the universal energy field and how to direct them to the patient. He can tell the difference between the energies in his own body and those being channelled from outside so that he does not deplete his own energies.

In the second process the healer reaches out to higher levels to create an energy link through which other entities may work. A temporary force field is built up around the healer and patient into which entities on other frequencies can act with complete freedom. These have come to be known as *spirit* helpers.[2] Those spirit helpers who act as teachers, often for the whole of a healer's life and beyond, are known as *guides*. The close relationship between guide and healer is based on a bond of love.

The healing guide or spirit guide is a person very similar in character to the healer so that they are compatible and can work in harmony. Apart from teaching and counselling the healer, the guide can ensure that the best resources are made available to him during the healing sessions. The guide also sets up suitable protective conditions around both healer and patient at these times.

The capacity to create an energy field where such highly skilled entities can operate gives the healer instant access to a range of treatments, covering any health condition. This is why most healers will treat whoever comes to them, with whatever condition, because experience has given them total confidence in their 'spirit helpers'.

The third process goes further than the cooperation and assistance of healing entities. When the healer is able to adjust the frequencies of his own body, healing entities can enter it and use all the healer's faculties. Again, such a capacity allows the healer to be quite confident of being able to treat whoever is brought to him.

Some healing entities have lived here on Earth during existences when they practised various forms of therapy. They have either gone on to master them to a high degree or undertaken further training on other levels of being. Some have never lived here. All of them have developed to the point where they can use their minds to direct the appropriate energies for the benefit of others. Many of them are doctors, therapists and surgeons who have continued to develop their knowledge after passing over and who wish to go on practising their skills. Love is the force which motivates any healing entity – love for mankind, animals or plants or the planet itself.

Some healers use one of the above ways of working, others use a combination. The important thing is for a healer to say 'yes' to being an instrument for healing. This means having and developing a love for all that exists and a strong desire to be of service. The healer becomes a channel to experience and to gain knowledge and it is only through working with patients that he will discover his part in the healing process. Many healers seem quite unaware of the methods being used to direct energy to their patients but, on other levels, they are perfectly aware of them.

Most healers do not try to predetermine the results of a treatment and only ask that what is right for the patient should take place. Some visualize the patient in a field of protection, radiating good health. This positive thought projection does much to support the patient on other levels, especially when physical problems persist.

UNDERSTANDING ILL-HEALTH

Healers do not diagnose a condition. Even after hearing a patient's description of symptoms and perhaps a medical diagnosis, the healer retains an open mind. This is because a condition is so often not what it seems to be and its cause may lie in some other area altogether. Experience shows that the healer's job is to heal the *patient* and not the condition alone.

Though it is the aim of healing to restore health at all times, the reasons for ill health must be taken into consideration. Spiritual healing does not see ill health as a problem to be wrestled with or as an evil to be fought against. Ill health is a condition, a state of affairs in an energy system which is drawing attention to an imbalance or disharmony in that system and those others which are related to it. (These systems will be discussed in detail in the next chapter.)

When disharmony is caused by the disconnection between our spiritual self and the personality expressing itself on the physical level – the person we see in the mirror – the disconnection is the problem which requires treatment. The physical, mental or emotional condition is the means of drawing our attention to this problem.

From a spiritual point of view, the meaning of 'cure' probably needs to be redefined. Healing seeks to clear up a condition whatever it might be. But healers are aware that patients may also be profoundly changed by the healing process and that for them the real cure may be an inner change. For many the inner change for the better has such a positive effect that the healing of their physical condition is of secondary importance. Since for many patients the change is so profound, the counselling element is such a vital part of the healing process.

Recognizing the condition as perhaps the catalyst to a positive reappraisal of ourselves and our lives allows a different perspective on ill health. The condition itself may be seen as an essential part of the process which leads to the cure.

Healing teaches that the condition has a valuable part to play. It is the converse of the normal situation where we are

22

encouraged to see a symptom as something to be rid of as quickly as possible so that we can get back to living our lives. It is not the healer's role to remove experiences which are needed for a patient's development. Rather, the healer can help each patient to come to terms with the experiences of ill health and to use them as an opportunity for progress.

In spiritual healing it is the progress towards self-integration which counts. Two powerful forces are released to bring this about. The first puts the patient back in touch with his higher self. The second gives the patient back control over his own life.

The release of these healing forces requires a willingness on the part of the patient to cooperate with them. No healer will work against a person's free will. When a patient decides to go to a healer, or asks someone to find out about healing for them, it is their higher self which is at work. The higher self directs the coming together of the patient and healer and forges the link with the energies of love.

READINESS FOR HEALING

A patient's unwillingness to go to a healer is a form of unreadiness. When he is not ready to make a link-up with his spiritual self healing may be prevented. Healing cannot take place because the condition is a sign of the need to bring the levels of being into harmony.

There are many forms of unreadiness. Sometimes the patient finds that his condition cannot be helped until he is willing to confront facets of his personality.

Case History: Simon was in his seventies and had chronic bronchitis. Six years before his consultation, he had been to a football match and got very wet. His cold developed into pneumonia. He was hospitalized and later released from hospital, but soon found he had bronchitis. His wife died shortly afterwards. Simon found he was unable to grieve; indeed, he was glad to see the back of her. His bronchitis grew worse and the hospital said that there was no chance of a recovery. All he could hope for was to keep the condition at its present level. He could walk slowly but could do nothing vigorous. He could no longer enjoy the company of women which made his life lonely and miserable. He was willing to try healing as a last resort but 'realized he was a hopeless case'.

At his first healing session he was told that there was no such thing as a hopeless case or an incurable condition but there were incurable patients. A number of spirit helpers came to work on him. His bronchial tubes were examined and congestion in the bottom of each lung noted. On examining his energy system he was found to have a blockage in the throat centre and an even more severe blockage in the heart centre. (See Chapter 3 for a description of energy centres and blockages.)

While work was done on his physical body his attention was drawn to the cause of the blockages. His relationship with his wife had been poor and had further deteriorated at the time of her death. He had felt hatred and, finally, indifference towards her. All this he had been unable to express and his feelings were choked back in his throat. He spoke of a coldness in the chest when he thought about her.

It was difficult to convince Simon that there was any connection between his blocked energy centres and his debilitating chest condition, but he said he was prepared to accept that it might be possible. There was unfinished business between him and his wife which had to be settled – resentments to be got rid of and lots of forgiveness all round. He was assured that he could resolve the conflicts with his wife even though she had passed over. This was more difficult for Simon to accept, especially as he hardly thought about her any more. He was not prepared to look into his heart at the bitterness and failure that lay there, exerting their relentless pressure on his life. Healing did improve his circulation however, and he was able to climb stairs and go out more.

In spite of these improvements he continually dismissed the painful memory of his wife from healing sessions. He was not ready to make the vital connection between his emotions and his lungs and had hoped that his problems could be cleared up

24

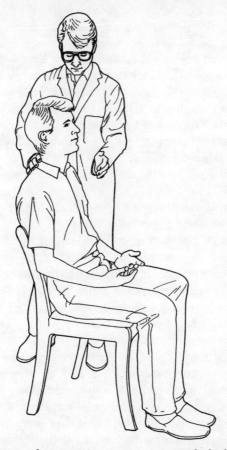

Fig. 3. Scanning the patient's energy system with the hand. Here the hand is held a few inches away from the throat chakra

by laying on of hands.

Simon's condition had not yet pushed him into a state of readiness to confront his deeper problems and energy blockages. Even though patients may see a healer, they may also put all kinds of blocks in the way to prevent healing from getting through. Since healing depends on the transmission of the correct energies, blockages may well prevent these transmissions to the patient's own energy system.

The Need for the Condition

People see themselves as hopeless cases or have been told they are. This is a powerful block set up by the mind. Some patients are still very sceptical; 'I've come but I don't expect it to work,' or 'Do your best, it's all mumbo jumbo anyway,' are phrases which signify a mental or emotional block.

Other patients seem to need their illness and after repeated treatments it becomes obvious that they do not really want to get better. There is always a reason for this if the healer looks carefully enough.

Case History: Maureen had been nursing her sick mother for years and the rest of the family were quite happy to let her get on with it. She had never married and saw that she had little hope of meeting anyone. She had been suffering from depression for a number of years and had become an outpatient at the local mental hospital. A nurse was brought in to cope when she had these bouts of illness. She refused to talk over the problem with the rest of the family.

Maureen needed counselling to improve her self-image and change her attitudes. She also needed healing on a mental and emotional level to raise her morale and improve her outlook. For some time, however, she continued to use the power of her mind to get sick until she found the strength to face her brothers and sisters and demand that they share in the care of their mother. In so doing she took another step towards taking control of her own destiny.

Destiny as a Factor

Another factor which healing cannot work against is a patient's destiny. Here, a patient may accept the healing but his higher self rejects it. This is because all healing is directly related to a person's reason for coming to this planet. They may have decided to experience certain conditions for their own learning purposes. Some souls even take on a condition so that they can teach others, either by the example they set in coping with it or through the experiences that other people undergo in caring for them.

Case History: Roger. When Roger was born he was a crumpled heap with little control over any part of his body. His parents were told that he would only live for a few months at the most. Nevertheless, he was given healing every week and continued to live past his first birthday. Today he is ten and zips around in a special motorized chair. His powerful will and difficult personality seem to give him the strength to cope with his disability. Healing helped the little person to survive against all odds and completely changed the lives of his parents, but it could not change the destinies of the three souls concerned to learn and grow through the life of Roger.

CONTROL

Many reasons for illness seem due to events over which we either have control or do not have it. Experiences like accidents, personal attack, the effects of pollution, war or infection seem to be out of our control. But records of healers' conversations with patients indicate that very often some part of ourselves is in control and exerts an influence which puts us in the right place at the right time to go through the unpleasant experience.

Psychologists and physicists say that we give meaning to coincidental events because their synchronicity affects us in some way. The psychoanalyst Jung felt that there was a force, such as the higher self, which directs such events so that they have meaning for those involved. Something may be learned through every experience. Even the most horrendous accidents have led to a change in people's lives for the better, plunging them into situations where they have to use skills or talents which had previously been hidden, drawing on resources which they may not have realized they possessed.

We can decide whether to smoke or overeat, whether to take exercise or drugs of any kind, and in this sense we could be said to be in control. But when we do anything to excess, neglect or abuse ourselves, control has been given up due to a disharmony or imbalance.

MIND AND EMOTIONS

The mind and the emotions have a powerful influence over how well we are in control of our lives. Events happen to people which leave such a mark that their patterns of thinking and feeling continually affect their behaviour in a negative way. Even though they may dislike what is going on, they cannot understand what is happening until they see the results. Such things are a cause of great unhappiness and people take all kinds of measures to cope with them.

Case History: Sylvia was a large lady who needed help with various aches and pains. These were quickly dealt with by the healer but, within a week or so, new ones appeared elsewhere. In counselling sessions she talked of her doting mother and drunken, bullying father. She had started eating to stifle the urge to cry and shout out her protests and she had been obese since puberty.

A scan of her energy system revealed long-standing blocks in the solar plexus, heart and throat centres. During the treatment on these centres her mother appeared to her inner vision but, at first, Sylvia could not confront her father in this way. The patient's higher self determines whether or not a person (who may be alive or passed over) appears on a subtle level. Healers are always thrilled when it does for it provides excellent evidence of the patient's needs and the way the treatment is progressing.

After a few healing sessions Sylvia was able to allow her father to come in and found she had gained the strength to deal with the unresolved conflicts with her parents. There was much sorrow, anger and bitterness and, again, forgiveness was a key to moving out of the cage of trapped emotions which she had built in order to survive.

Sylvia needed healing on all levels and support to break the habit of constantly feeding herself. Gradually she regained control over her mind and emotions. She realized her body had helped her in alerting her to the situation and this realization gave her a new respect for herself.

Illness as a Cry for Help

Illness is often a cry for help and it is a tribute to the human mind that it can create a seemingly incurable condition in order to command the attention of others.

Case History: Harriet was a healthy seven-year-old who enjoyed her days at school. Her parents objected to aspects of the school's policy and sent her to another one much further from her home. Soon after this she was taken ill. The doctor could not find out what was wrong with her. The following day she lost the use of her legs and was rushed into hospital. She continued to deteriorate and a friend of the family asked for distant healing to be sent.

It seemed the child's main problem was her change of school and the emotional trauma she had suffered as a result. Healing was sent to Harriet and her unhappy parents. A few days later she began to perk up and her parents visited the hospital to tell her that they had decided to let her go back to her old school. She continued to recover and the hospital discharged her, informing her parents that she had been suffering from a 'mystery virus'.

The lesson for all concerned was to respect the spirit of the child as much as the adult. The child has a mind and emotions of a power equal to any adult. What they have not yet learned as children is how to control, develop and use these forces to create a better life for themselves.

Distant Healing

In Harriet's case, distant healing was quite effective in reaching her mind and helping to allay her fears and calm her emotions. Distant or absent healing is used to send healing energies to a patient when it is not possible for them to get to a healer. This may be due to distance or lack of time or the inability of the person to travel.

Studies show that in most cases the process is as effective as hands-on healing. There are obvious circumstances, however, when the patient needs the reassurance of the healer's presence or when counselling or explanation are an important element in the treatment.

Distant healing may be sent anywhere on the planet; distance is no object since the healing is either being directed by the mind energy of the healer or is being transmitted on a level of being outside the physical plane. In both cases there is no limitation placed on the movement of healing energies until they enter the patient's own energy system.

Healing prayers work in a similar way and can be sent out by anyone. Unfortunately, so many well-meaning prayers ask for a specific outcome and the energy which projects them is too often negative. This cannot be used for healing. We do not know what is best for another person, only their higher self knows this. Healers find it more effective to send out a thought of love and protection to the patient, visualizing them surrounded by a cocoon of pure light and leaving the outcome to higher forces. The love energy projected can then be used by healing entities to help those who have been mentioned.

Healers usually have long lists of people and these lists are offered up in this way with thoughts of love and light and that what is best for the patient should be the outcome.

Some healers have the ability to project themselves in their subtle body to the location of the patient; they give the healing in the same way as if they were physically present. During any healing session, subtle energy first enters the subtle body of a person, before it flows into the physical, so that this way of working is just as effective.

Other healers have the capacity to create a force field where the patient can be brought to them or travel to them in their subtle body. Again, healing takes place on this level.

Sometimes patients are aware of these events and report having 'dreams' in which a person gives them healing or assures them that everything is going to be all right. At no point do they feel afraid.

The Power of Thought

There is no limit to the power of the mind – only that which we put on it. Similarly, emotions are a force on all levels. Such tremendous forces can be directed by the human will towards others to achieve positive or negative aims. They are energies whose force is determined by the inner power of the person projecting them.

Healers frequently have to explain to patients that thoughts become things. Positive thoughts become positive things and negative ones likewise. This is why it is so important what we think and feel. A hateful or aggressive thought about someone immediately enters their energy field. If such thoughts are about society, institutions, a country or group, they coalesce with others generally to lower the vibrations around us and other people.

Equally destructive is the power of the mind or the emotions when turned in on ourselves. We hear the phrases: 'eaten up with jealousy', 'tortured by remorse', 'locked into grief' and so on, illustrating the mind power we can unleash to destroy our lives.

Case History: Wayne was a lively, bouncing boy whose vigorous personality irritated his mother to distraction. She bellowed at him and chastised him and told him she could not love him if he behaved like this. Around eight years of age he began to show signs of arthritis in his joints and by eighteen needed to have a hip replacement. The medical profession had done their best to help him.

When Wayne went for healing in his late twenties he was sobbing with anger and fear over the pain and disablement that had come upon him. His energy system had a severe blockage in the heart centre. He was guided by the healer to repair the damage to the centre and release the energies that were now working against him. He cried bitterly as his mother appeared to him in a meditation to explain that he had found a brilliant way of being a 'good boy' – by locking his joints with arthritis. Now they were deformed and hardly functioning. He needed healing to release the lifetime of anger and resentment which he felt against so many people. It took months to help him realize that he no longer needed the condition and that it need not be permanent.

POSITIVE SIDE EFFECTS

But healers are well aware that people do not always want to confront themselves in the way that Wayne did. Healers never force a patient into this position. Most patients simply want relief from a painful or trying symptom. If this is all they ask of the healer he will do his best to bring this about. Nevertheless, healing at this level may often filter through to affect other levels so that a pain is cured at the same time as a change in attitude is brought about.

Case History: Peter had spent his working life as a miner during which time he became trapped under a fall of rock. His hearing v. as damaged and his back suffered severe bruising but he had no trouble with it for ten years until chronic back pain led to his retirement. Peter tried healing as a last resort but lost his scepticism when a growth on his hip, which he had not mentioned, disappeared after the first treatment. Soon he found his hearing improving along with the back problem.

Peter decided to keep an open mind about spiritual healing but at no time did he wish to discuss it. His wife reported that he had become more considerate towards her than he had ever been and was making a strong effort to control his irritable temperament. For her these welcome side-effects were the added benefits she came to experience over the months of Peter's treatment.

Much of the counselling side of any healing treatment will involve helping patients to understand how they have used their mind or emotions against themselves – and how to reverse this trend. Many people find it difficult to accept that a beneficial outcome may arise from the experience of illness. But patients often describe how ill health has changed their lives for the better or made them 'better people'. This is because they have been forced to confront themselves and to look at themselves dispassionately.

HEALING OPERATIONS

Case History: Yolanda. When Yolanda tried spiritual healing, she had already investigated many forms of complementary therapy and had benefited from each one. She felt that each time her condition had led her to the therapy and that she had found herself making new discoveries as a result of her investigations.

Yolanda had been a fast-living accountant in Australia and felt that she had abused her body in many ways. She had had a number of relationships, including two marriages. A wrong diagnosis led to a hysterectomy and the wound healed very badly. She also had a second operation in the same area which failed to heal. For years she had coped with the effects of her two operations, determined to find a cure. Healing not only led her gladly to face issues within herself but gave her a new interest in complementary medicine.

She insisted that her painful condition had led her away from a lifestyle which was destroying her and had pushed her towards a greater understanding of herself and those around her. It also gave her the compassion to help other people to regain their health.

Yolanda may have gained many new insights into herself and found new interests to follow up, but she still needed a good surgeon to tidy up the damage in her groin. She refused to go into hospital again so a healing 'operation' was called for. She was told what would probably happen and that she would feel very little or nothing at all – certainly not any pain. Yolanda laughed and said she was 'ready for anything!'.

She lay on the couch and relaxed. In a moment, two healing entities came in to carry out the work. Both had been surgeons in a past life but the techniques they used are as yet unavailable in hospitals. One of them directed a thin beam of energy to the

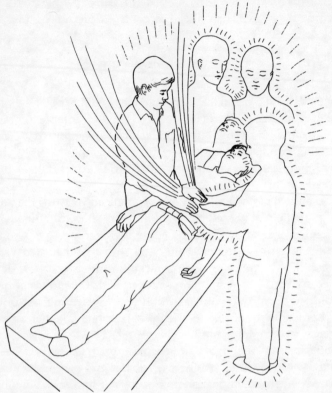

Fig.4. Spirit surgery: the healer holds his hands near the patient's abdomen while a spirit surgeon performs an operation. At one point the patient is 'out of his body', aided by spirit helpers

damaged area; this seemed to act as an anaesthetic. They were able to operate from inside the body and use special materials like plasters to hold tissues in place until they grew together properly.

Meanwhile, the whole of the pelvis was flooded in an orange glow. Yolanda said she could feel sensations, like movements, which were not unpleasant. When the operation was completed her whole body was surrounded by a cocoon of light for her protection. During the operation, Yolanda had been slightly 'out of her body' so she needed time to come

34

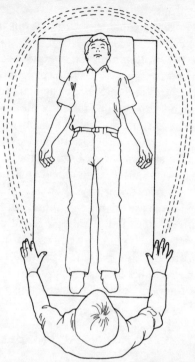

Fig.5. After healing, this patient's aura is sealed with a shell of protective golden energy (seen from above)

back into it and regain full awareness before she was allowed to stand up. While she was still lying down she was told by the healing entities that she no longer needed the condition and that it would clear up.

Healers are used to this kind of operation being performed on a patient when necessary and know that it is a natural part of healing. If a job needs to be done the healer can call on the services of experts and techniques to deal with any condition. Only the healer himself imposes limits on his capabilities.

Such operations are known erroneously as 'psychic' operations – having been given the label when anything supernormal was classified as 'psychic'. 'Psychic' surgery does not depend on the psychic abilities of the healer, rather on his ability to

35

remove himself from the scene and to create an energy field in which other entities, capable of carrying out the operation, can work.

In places like the Philippines such operations are carried out in much the same way as that on Yolanda except that the healer puts his hands on the patient's body, appears to open it and removes tissue where this is called for. This method is part of the accepted cultural tradition. The blood that always accompanies the operation is a sign to the patient and onlookers that it actually took place and was not a form of 'magic'.[3]

In western culture such signs meet with ridicule and suspicion and do not occur, neither are they necessary. Whether these signs are always genuine, is, in any case, debatable. During spiritual healing growths and other pathological materials are reduced to substances which can be discarded by the patient via the body's normal elimination systems. This is what occurs during the removal, for example, of tumours or other cancerous tissue.

HEALING OF 'MENTAL PROBLEMS'

When patients can see or feel the disappearance of their condition, their sense of relief is immediate. It may be more difficult for someone with a mental or nervous illness to imagine that healing has anything to offer them. Their suffering is internal and very often their condition is 'invisible' to those who are not aware of their problem.

Spiritual healing has a great deal to offer those with a mental or nervous illness, as well as those with phobias, allergies, skin problems and the whole range of conditions termed 'mental illness'. As already explained, healing works on all levels of a person so that much can be done to help a patient to rehabilitate.

Unfortunately, there are many people in mental hospitals who are not able to respond to medical treatment and who desperately need some other kind of help. Some of these patients are experiencing subtle energetic phenomena but they do not know anyone who understands what is happening to them or who can explain it.

Abilities, such as clairvoyance or clairaudience, occur more widely than we realize. Most people are reluctant to admit experiences of subtle energies for fear of ridicule or worse. Many patients have had a lifetime of experiences which have ensured their admittance to mental hospitals. Here they have been submitted to drug and electrical therapy and, finally, diagnosed as schizophrenic. A healer can tell at the first consultation whether this is the case or not.

When 'hearing things', 'seeing things' or 'sensing things' are simply other names for a well-developed high sense perception then the person is perfectly well and does not need to be hospitalized. Instead, he needs support and guidance to accept and develop his abilities if he so wishes.

High sense perception (HSP) is a natural ability which all of us possess to a greater or lesser degree. It allows us to be aware of vibrations outside the physical level. In some people the critical faculty of the intellect intervenes to prevent them from accepting what these perceptions are telling them. Intuition, a common example of HSP in action, is closer to the surface in a greater number of women than men. A fuller discussion of HSP follows in Chapter 3.

DEALING WITH STRESS

People who have been through various forms of therapy and still fell unwell often have to contend with the added burden of stress which remaining unwell has given them. Healing can quickly induce a state of tranquillity in a patient and many healers are happy to help him discover what is causing the stress. The healer can then suggest a programme of stress elimination or stress management, as the case may be.

Case History: Gervaise thought he would try some healing because his wife had been to a health exhibition and had felt a profound sense of relaxation after only a fifteen-minute session. This feeling lasted for a further week during which she also felt more positive about a family problem which had been worrying her and about life in general. Gervaise thought there was little wrong with him, apart from a few aches, but he had recently had flu and felt the need for a general tone-up. Healing is able to do this by balancing the patient's energy system and giving him an energy boost. Gervaise was surprised when his left leg was revealed as still causing a blockage at certain energy points. He said he had badly broken his shin during a skiing accident. Then the aches down his right side were dealt with, particularly his shoulder. He was a newspaper cameraman and was used to carrying all his equipment on one shoulder. His left leg had been trying to compensate for this imbalance and this, he revealed, was the ache which had reluctantly brought him to see a healer.

Gervaise need to learn how to relax in his hectic job and the healing session ended with a lesson in how to let go totally, physically and mentally.

CHILDREN AND HEALING

Children have no problem in letting go and usually thoroughly enjoy a healing session. In law a child must first be taken to a doctor if he is unwell, but parents should realize that children respond to healing in the same way that adults do. They also have an added advantage in presenting fewer barriers to healing.

Teachers who are aware of the *human energy field* (HEF) notice how young children at school are aware of it too. They like to show it round the people they draw and to put in the different colours they see.

Case History: Tracey was born prematurely and had poor coordination on one side of her body. She had been a regular visitor to the clinic in the early months of her life and her parents decided to ask for healing for her when she was six years old. She wanted to show the healer a picture of her mother talking to the headmistress which she had drawn that day. A pink cloud entirely surrounded her mother but the headmistress had a grey one around her. Asked why the colours were different for the two women, Tracey explained: 'Mummy usually looks like that, Miss Hillman was in a bad mood today.'

Tracey had noticed how the energy aura around people changed according to their mood. Quite naturally she assumed that everybody else did too. During healing sessions she would look up at the light surrounding her and at the healing entities who came in to work on her body.

High sense perception is very close to the surface of consciousness in young children. Tracey was so relaxed that she was able to express what she was sensing. She took great delight in turning to her mother to describe what she was seeing which the healer was able to corroborate.

Children are spirits with a physical body and only the size of their form makes them smaller than adults. Adults who fail to grasp this think that children do not understand what is going on around them and that the problems confronting parents have no meaning for the children. But once it is remembered that they, too, are spirit, adults are able to realize why children do suffer physically, mentally and emotionally through what is happening in their lives. So often this is not revealed until they grow up and try to live their adult lives, only to find the scars of the past rising at last to the surface.

ANIMAL HEALING

Animals are a form of spirit and enjoy healing. Many vets work with healers and in parts of the USA it is legal to run healing clinics for animals. Many healers there have responded to the need for animal healing and have had to specialize in a particular animal because of the demand for their services.

The energy field of the animal tells the healer whether it is balanced physically, mentally and spiritually. As in the life of a human being, whatever surrounds an animal, whatever happens to it, are energy inputs which are just as important as their food and drink. All life conditions contribute to the balance or imbalance of any animal, as they do to us.

ATTITUDES TO HEALING

Spiritual healing has tended to be the therapy of last resort. The patient has tried everything else so what is there to lose? This attitude has put an unfair burden of proof on healing. If it works there is belief and euphoria. If it does not, disbelief and scepticism are reinforced.

Under such circumstances, a patient with a serious or long-standing condition has energy imbalances which have gained such a hold that conventional medicine has little or nothing to offer. Further, medication or treatment may have been tried whose side-effects have caused additional damage.

By this stage, the patient's mental and emotional attitudes are having negative effects on the condition as well. For example, the patient feels he probably cannot, or will not, get better – a message which is continually transmitted to the healing forces of the body.

In extreme cases, damage is so severe that the body has difficulty in supporting the subtler energy systems which are keeping it 'alive'. This is when a condition is diagnosed as terminal.

All these changes in the patient's energy patterns will have to be dealt with by the healer and the healing energies that he can channel.

Happily, as the records of healers the world over will testify, thousands of patients have totally recovered from grave illnesses while others have been greatly helped to cope with them. If this were not so, spiritual healing would have disappeared long ago.

Healing is being recognized by a growing number of people today, not as a last resort but as a first step in restoring harmony and regaining control over one's health. It is not an alternative but a therapy in its own right – one which is entirely complementary to any other which a person may require. As its boundaries are being pushed back, the state of the art and science of spiritual healing is changing all the time. We are still in the process of finding out what healing can do and, as we discover more about healing, so we are discovering more about ourselves and our place in the scheme of things.

Spiritual healing reveals that our deepest need is to realize who we are – a spirit in a physical body – and to let our spirit through to illuminate our lives. Our spirit is the sun of our being. Life without its spiritual dimension would be like living under perpetual cloud where the vitalizing rays of the sun have long been forgotten. There would be no life here on Earth without the energy of the sun and there would be no life within us without the energy of the spirit.

Subtle energy is constantly available to us in the universal energy field as an energy of love and healing. As people create new health problems, so healing always presents the loving response. The knowledge and wisdom, derived from the compassionate practice of spiritual healing, is helping to lay the foundation for the new science of Subtle Energy Medicine.

3

The Human Energy Field

A S LIGHT passes through a droplet of water it is split into a spectrum of colours – the colours of the rainbow. The water droplet, acting like a prism, shows us the colours contained within the light. The human spirit, like a ray of light, passes through the experiences of life, throwing off a spectrum of colours which reveals the levels of existence.

There are three main levels of being to explain the process of healing – *physical*, *etheric* and *spiritual*. Each level of a human being gives off energy so that a resonating field of energy totally surrounds the body. It is this combined emanation which makes the human rainbow, the aura or the human energy field (HEF). Some healers claim to see seven or more layers or levels within the aura, each with its own colour.

As we begin to explore the energy field we find that the whole body gives off energy generally and at specific points in particular. Most of us are aware, for example, that hands give off energy.

When the two hands are brought together slowly, this energy can be felt more and more intensely. If the experiment is done with another person by holding the hand near them, the same phenomenon is experienced. Another person's energy field can be sensed in many different ways. High sense perception allows us to see, feel, hear or be aware of it in other ways. We are aware if someone is close behind us or watching us because HSP tells us. The energies in some

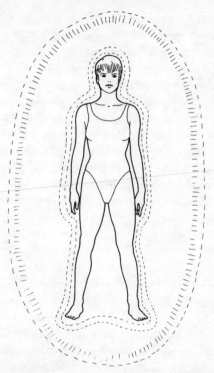

Fig. 6. Some healers see the aura as 'layers' of light and colour. Here four 'bodies' or layers are seen in the HEF

people's fields are so intense that they are easily picked up by others who may be attracted or repelled by them.

When we meet someone new we tend to like or dislike them straightaway, but we cannot explain why. This is because we respond to their energy field in a positive or negative way. Everything about another person, including their life experiences, is stored in the energy field. This enables those with a developed HSP to 'tune in' and extract whatever they wish. But we are all sensitive in this sense to a greater or lesser degree and are gaining impressions of people and places during every moment of the encounter.

The human energy field also presents an up-to-date record

of a person's health. Healers tend to be very sensitive to this aspect of a patient's aura and it enables them to empathize with their condition straight away. This is why some healers complain of feeling the same pain, the same nausea or constriction in the chest and so on. They are simply blending their aura with the patient's as part of the linking process described in the previous chapter.

The HEF, then, is the total energy pattern of a patient. It is not just their body but the whole person, including the spirit within them. This is where healing begins and ends. The HEF indicates why healing may be necessary and provides a living energy record which can monitor the treatment being given. Finally, it tells accurately of the patient's return to balance and harmony.

BIO-ENERGY AND KIRLIAN PHOTOGRAPHY

The presence of a bio-energy field or aura around living things was discounted by science because it could not be detected by current technology. Then in the 1890s a Polish nobleman, Yakub Yodko-Narkevitch, began investigating corona-discharge photography by using a high voltage, high frequency electric charge instead of light. He recorded differences in the electro-magnetic field between a healthy person and a sick person, between sleeping or wakefulness. He drew attention to the fact that physiological and psychological changes in a person could be monitored using this new technique.

With the Russian Revolution his findings were lost until the technique was rediscovered by Semyon Kirlian in 1939. A similar charge was passed across a film on which certain biological specimens had been placed and strange light patterns occured around these specimens. No light source was used and yet a corona of energy showed up each time.

Corona-discharge photography (or Kirlian photography as it is also called) was classified as secret by the Soviet government until 1960 when Kirlian published a report with his wife, Valentina. The Kirlians claimed that the corona discharge was the scientific evidence of the existence of a bio-energy field or aura. Their report created tremendous interest in scientific circles worldwide. Clairvoyants saw it as proof of what they had always been perceiving through HSP.

Researchers went on to discover that the light given out by a subject varied according to the vital force present. A leaf plucked straight from a tree showed an energy field which got smaller as the leaf dried out. The corona around a healthy leaf was markedly different to that around leaves taken from infected plants. Not surprisingly, photographs of healers' hands showed a significant increase in the energy being given off when healing was being given.

The Russian experiments were extended, there and in the West, to objects such as coins, pieces of metal and rock, which showed that everything is surrounded by an energy field.

In view of their discoveries, Russian scientists put forward the theory of a 'bioplasmic' field emanating from, and surrounding, all living material. Kirlian photography has further shown that there seems to be an 'invisible' matrix or energy blueprint inherent in every living thing. Photographs of leaf sections, for example, always show the full outline of the leaf before it was cut (the 'phantom leaf' effect). Photographs of people with missing fingers or limbs also show the energy matrix as complete which supports the findings of clairvoyants and healers that there is a complete blueprint of the physical body existing at a higher frequency (the etheric level).

As the Kirlians and other researchers have found, the corona around living material differs in many ways to that of inorganic subjects. Even allowing for chemical, and therefore atomic, differences there seems to be some added energy ingredient to account for this. Healers would say that this is the vitality energy or life force, a special energy which is only present in living things.

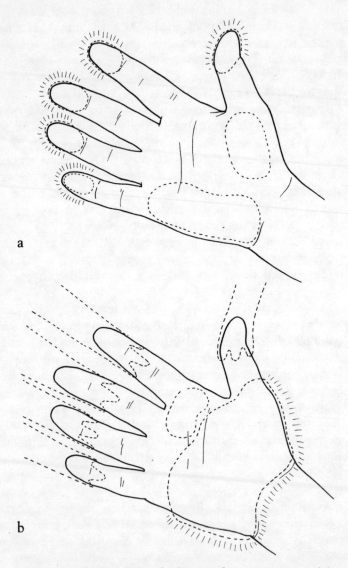

Fig. 7. Healer's right hand, showing the energy corona (a) before healing (b) during a healing session (based on Kirlian photography)

VITALITY ENERGY

Most of us are affected by climatic conditions without realizing the reason for our change of mood. On a sunny day when the sky is blue we tend to feel vitalized and more optimistic. On grey days we may feel less energetic or even depressed (Seasonal Affective Disorder (SAD) syndrome.) This is not simply due to the effects of light intensity upon us for these conditions also affect the amount of vitality energy available to us in the *universal energy field* (UEF). Clear days increase the flow whereas cloud reduces it.

Vitality energy moves in and out of the body without our conscious knowledge unless its depletion tells us we are exhausted. In a healthy person the amount of life force is balanced and in harmony with the rest of his energy systems. This vitality energy was known to the ancient Indians as *prana* and the science of controlled breathing to increase one's vitality or energy level is known as *pranayama*.

Many ancient cultures have known of these concepts and their findings are recorded as part of oral tradition or in their literature. In India, the Sanskrit language developed a vocabulary which encompasses a range of scientific, religious and philosophical concepts in one coherent system. In this vocabulary, single words may be used to signify whole concepts. During the first three decades of this century, when writers came into contact with the Indian yoga schools, they realized the convenience of using Sanskrit terms to describe their research and experiences. Many Sanskrit words, like 'yoga', have now become part of the vocabulary of most modern languages. Pranayama is an important element in the yoga system of exercises.

Globules of vitality energy can be seen in the air against a clear blue sky as quickly moving black dots. We need energy from the sun, air, water and food and there are biological systems in the physical body to deal with these energies and make them available for our use. But we also need other energies, such as vitality energy, which have a source outside the physical solar system. Again, the human form is designed so that these may be absorbed and used.

THE ETHERIC BODY AND THE CHAKRAS

Interpenetrating the physical body is a more subtle body vibrating at a higher frequency. This second body has come to be known as the *etheric* body, from the ancient Greek term which referred to the upper regions of the atmosphere or heaven as ether. Seers of the time had witnessed that, on passing over, people carried on living in their 'heavenly' or etheric body.

The etheric body contains an energy blueprint upon which the physical body is shaped and anchored. This means that it is closely linked to the physical. It contains the structures which allow us to absorb high frequency energy of various kinds, including the vital force. It processes them and passes them into the physical. The etheric structures were seen by Indian seers (*rishis*) as bell-shaped appendages with stems connecting them to points on the spine. The rishis called them *chakras* (wheels) since their insides seemed like whirling vortices of light with 'spokes' radiating out from a central point. These are the force centres or 'energy centres' of the human body. The Chinese call them *dantian*. These centres allow energy to flow in and out and they contain regulating mechanisms to control this flow.

The tubular stems of the chakras are joined to an etheric channel next to the spine. This channel links the chakras and allows incoming energy at one chakra to be processed and sent to another. As the flow moves upwards through the etheric channel, the energies become increasingly refined. The linkage points also provide ways into the physical body, via the endocrine glands, where incoming energies have an important effect on the surrounding organs.

The location of the chakras is the most common method of naming tham. Readers may find differing versions of the names, and even their locations, in different books on the

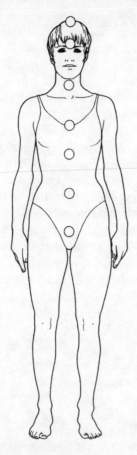

Fig. 8. *The seven main energy centres (chakras)*

subject. It is more important to know that they exist and to back this up with personal experience.

The Base or Root Chakra is at the base of the spine. It absorbs energy from the planet and processes issues concerned with basic instincts, survival, and physical perceptions. Its energies impact on the physical body via the adrenal glands.

The Sacral Chakra is just below the navel, It absorbs vitality energy and is concerned with creativity, sexuality and the inner child. It is linked to the physical via the sex glands.

49

The Solar Plexus Chakra is just below the breast bone and diaphragm. It absorbs vitality energy and is concerned with the mind and emotions. This accounts for the link between mind and emotions in human life. Here, negative energies such as fear and anxiety are processed. It is linked to the physical via the Islets of Langerhans glands in the pancreas.

The Heart Chakra, in the centre of the chest, is concerned with all aspects of love in our life, including compassion and empathy. It is linked to the physical via the thymus gland.

The Throat Chakra is concerned with all forms of expression and communication. It links to the physical via the thyroid gland.

The Brow Chakra, in the middle of the brow, is concerned with high sense perception and intuition. It is linked to the physical via the hypothalamus and pituitary gland.

The Crown Chakra, on the top of the head, is concerned with all issues of spirituality and our link with the Source. It connects with the physical via the pineal gland.

Links Between the Chakras

There are links between the chakras which affect everybody and are particularly relevant to people in certain professions. The link between the sacral and throat chakras, for instance, is important to any artist or performer. This is the energy link that joins the forces of creative joy (the sacral chakra) to the forces of creative expression (the throat chakra).

Case History: Charles was a musician who came for healing because of a back problem. Standing to play in sessions had aggravated a weakness in his back but healing revealed more than this. A scan of his energy field showed that energy was not moving from his sacral chakra to the throat chakra, neither was it being properly used in the latter chakra. Between them was the heart chakra where a further blockage was discovered.

Counselling sessions enabled Charles to understand what was going on in his life and why his stage performances were not 'up to scratch'. He was having problems with a love relationship. He also felt he would like to have a better relationship with his parents. Childhood experiences seemed to have 'locked him up'. Charles had been storing up tension and stress in his lower back which gave way under the strain which his work imposed. Some of the stress was due to his relationships and some due to his awareness of his poor performances as a musician. Once he had been for a few treatments, Charles became aware of the energy links in his body and how they affected his work. He was able to feel the difference as energy moved once again through his heart, throat and sacral chakras and his colleagues could appreciate the results.

The Heart Chakra

The key energy block being encountered by healers today is in the heart chakra, the seat of love, compassion and the expression of the higher emotions. For human life to progress to the next stage, the heart chakra must be unblocked and the energy of love allowed to flow in and out unimpeded.

The chakra above it, the throat, is the energy focus of expression and communication so that if the heart chakra is blocked every creative act is stunted as Charles, the musician, found out. Intellectual ideas and mental creations which gain their power from the solar plexus will likewise fail to find their true expression. Perhaps most important of all is the expression of love. The heart's impulse must rise towards the crown where it becomes an outpouring of love towards all creation. On the way it demonstrates its healing power in all forms of loving expression through the throat chakra.

51

Healers know, through working with patients, that the energies of the heart chakra are exerting an unrelenting force on humanity. This manifests in our questioning of love, sex and affairs of the heart; the function of marriage and the family; whether to extend the hand of help or friendship; realizing our inability to love ourselves. Where our bodies are concerned, the pressure manifests as problems of heart disease, coronary breakdown and diseases of the chest. The heart chakra also draws attention to the misery and disease brought about by the denial of love, the lack of love, the substitutes for love, the giving of hatred, the abundance of anger and despair and the abusive approach to all facets of human life.

The heart chakra stands midway between physical and spiritual life. It is the chakra where both forms of energy are processed. Spiritual energy moving downwards may be blocked by the heart. This will deny the lower three chakras the vital energies needed for preparing the human body for personal transformation.

Symbolically, the heart chakra represents this crucial point of balance and transformation. The human being is subject to two main pressures – to its physical self (the ego) and to its higher self, the link with the Source of all. But our purpose is to express the spirit through the physical, to illuminate physical matter.

If we imagine the two forces of spirit and matter moving towards each other through the chakras, the heart chakra is where they meet (Fig. 9a). When this chakra is functioning in harmony with the rest of the energy systems, the two forces are able to blend. The transformed energies continue on their journey through the chakras where they will manifest in the relevant areas of life (Fig. 9b). This figure symbolically represents the integrated human being who has created a way of life by which the spirit can find satisfactory expression.

Open and Closed Chakras

The chakras extend to all levels of a person's being. They contain valve-like structures which are open or closed according to a person's stage of development. This determines how

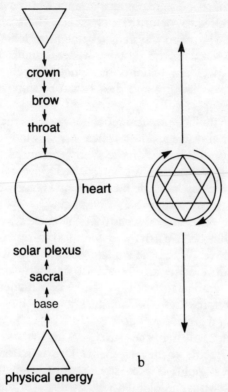

Fig. 9. *The two forces of spirit and matter (a) flow towards the heart chakra and (b) the energies blend here before continuing on their journey of transformation through the chakras*

many levels of energy can enter a chakra. Since most energy input comes in the form of psychological material the chakra mechanisms ensure that we are only conscious of incoming energies with which we can deal.

All chakras are open at the level nearest the physical to facilitate the flow of vitality energy to both physical and etheric systems. At these levels there can be no such thing as a 'closed' chakra since the physical, without the input of the life force, would soon break down and disintegrate – as it does at the time of death.

Healers sometimes encounter patients who have practised special exercises to 'open their chakras'. These are designed to open up the energy system to the next level and were originally devised in the East for students under competent supervision. Modern patients have needed help when this supervision was lacking and they began to suffer unpleasant side-effects.

These can include physical problems as well as acute mental and emotional distress. The application of drugs to sedate or calm the patient is helpful in the short term but, sooner rather than later, the damage must be repaired. Medical treatment given with the best possible motives may even exacerbate the patient's problems rather than solve them.

What occurs in such cases is that the chakra 'valve' to the next level has been partially or fully forced open as a result of the exercises. When the student has not reached the level of spiritual development to be able to deal with the inrush of new and unfamiliar material – energies of a higher frequency and greater force than previously known – he experiences imbalance and great discomfort.

So a healer will help the patient to understand that there are no short cuts to development. Life is so ordered that the correct stimulus is provided at the correct moment to ensure our spiritual unfoldment. Many illnesses and traumatic incidents are thus stepping stones to evolution and progress.

Closing Down

Healers are also asked to help deal with the detrimental effects on people who have been told to 'close down' certain chakras. It is extremely difficult to do this but it is possible to create energy blocks in those areas through the mental pressure to 'close' them. When it is realized that the subtle energy system is the life support of the physical, it is obvious that the chakras are designed to be permanent energy receivers and it is vital that they remain open and clear. As already explained, energy blocks lead to ill health and in no way provide any form of 'protection' for a person.

The problem has come about through confusing the aura with the energy centres. Once a healer has finished working he first clears his aura by mentally washing it with a clearing energy (such as the colour silver). Then he 'closes down' by mentally putting an energy shield or field of protection around his aura to prevent further input, absorption or loss of energies. This process also protects the healer against negative energies.

People complain of feeling drained after time spent amongst others, after shopping trips or journeys on public transport. This is often because they are in an 'open' state. A person who is depleted will unconsciously draw on this available energy source to bring about balance in his system (Figure 10).

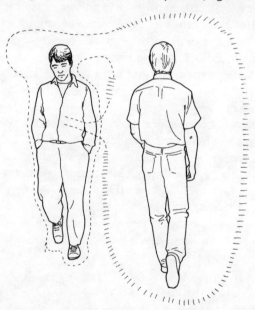

Fig. 10. The law of energy in action: the unfit person on the left has a lopsided aura and draws energy from the healer on the right as they pass in the street. The unfit person is unconsciously trying to balance his energy field by drawing in energy at the head and solar plexus. The healer has allowed this to happen by forgetting to close down and protect is own aura.

Chakra Colours

Certain energies are associated with each chakra and healers have seen how they manifest as different colours. Clairvoyants seem to agree on these colours, but readers will find varying descriptions of them. Ultimately, a person's own experience is the best guide. The colours are used as a chakra reference but this does not mean that they are the only colours which are seen at these points. Each chakra is related to an aspect of human life and a level of being which occur in energy terms as colour.

The basal chakra is associated with the colour red or deep pink; the sacral chakra with orange; the solar plexus with yellow; the heart with green, the colour of balance; the throat with sky blue; the brow with indigo and the crown with violet – the colours of the visible spectrum.

There is a chakra above the head which is associated with the colour white. Some writers use this as the colour for the crown chakra.

Because of their associations, the energies used for a particular condition may manifest as a similar colour. For example, the heart may need an energy which appears green, the uterus orange, the larynx blue, and so on. But a problem in a certain area may not need that colour of energy. Neither will a specific organ or condition require the same designated colour in every case. Every person's energy field is unique and the causes of the same disease in one person may be quite different in another.

THE AURA

The uniqueness of each person's energy field is revealed, to those with a developed HSP, in the aura – the emanation of light from within. The average person has an aura which appears to project as a light, smoky emanation a few inches beyond the edge of the body.

Spiritually developed people tend to have a very bright, clear aura which seems to project a little further than average, especially around the head. This accounts for the halo of light seen around saints and holy people which has been indicated by artists in their portrayal of such subjects.

The avatar, Sathya Sai Baba, who lives in India at the present time, has been the subject of many scientific investigations and has been a source of wonder to those who specialize in the human aura. The energy field around Sai Baba is so extensive that he cannot be considered human in this sense. Among hundreds of testimonies, that of Dr Frank Baranowski, a scientist from Arizona, is particularly striking.

Baranowski has been able to see auras since childhood and is interested in Kirlian photography as a method of recording them. Hearing of the profusion of holy men in India he went there to research their auras. He was disappointed until he met Sai Baba in 1978. Baranowski says:

The colour pink, rarely seen, typifies selfless love. This was the colour that Sai Baba had around him. The aura went beyond the building against which he stood; this energy field reached 30 to 40 feet in all directions.

Later, addressing college students at Brindavan, he said:

The aura Swami [Sai Baba] projected was not that of a man! The white was more than twice the size of any man's; the blue (spirituality) was practically limitless; and then there were gold and silver bands beyond even those, far beyond this building, right up to the horizon.

Baranowski has admitted to audiences all over the world that, as a scientist, he cannot account for his observations except that he is convinced that Sai Baba is the Creator, living now upon the planet. Perhaps it is not surprising that so many healers and clairvoyants have witnessed his presence during healing sessions.

Interpreting the Aura

Energies from outside a person, and changes brought about from within through physical, mental, emotional or spiritual activities, all leave an impression on an individual's energy patterns. The aura is the sum total of these effects which may be seen as various colours or felt as various intensities. But the amount of information which a person's aura may present to a healer depends on the healer's development and abilities. Some healers see the human aura as a single colour while others see many layers and the colours within these layers.

One of the most valuable faculties a healer may possess is to translate information in the aura into a picture of the patient's true condition. The information may include levels outside the physical which are, therefore, outside space/time. This makes it possible for a healer with well-developed HSP to perceive past events or traumas which have a bearing on the patient's current state of health.

Past events and traumas leave their energy traces on the structure of the human energy field (HEF), just as current energy transactions are doing. When scanning or examining the structure of a patient's HEF, the healer's ability to understand what he is sensing is a useful diagnostic tool. This understanding can not only locate the energy traces which are causing a blockage, but later confirm whether treatment has removed them.

Because the whole human body is a receiver of energy, we also need to be aware of how others and the outside world are affecting us – how much we can control and what measures to take with energies we cannot control. This is where the mind and the emotions have an important impact on our lives and our health. Energy blocks and imbalance were mentioned earlier as the cause of much physical ill health. Because the mental and emotional aspects of life are present at all levels, disorders can occur there too.

THE EFFECTS OF NEGATIVE THOUGHTS AND FEELINGS

Thoughts and feelings have a direct bearing on the HEF because they are energies. They interact with our energy systems to change them in a positive or negative way – bringing about balance or imbalance. We are affected by our own thoughts and feelings and we experience the effects in the relevant chakra. For example, if we are anxious or in a panic we may feel 'butterflies in the stomach'. Such energies accumulate in the subtle energy system. If they were positive, they would have helped the flow of energy. But negative energies create a blockage which leads to such feelings as a queasy stomach. When these accumulations continue to occur over a period of time, sooner or later physical organs or systems are affected – the body's way of alerting us to the problem.

Case History: Robert. When Robert came for healing he had already been to the hospital with a suspected gastric ulcer and was having to take doses of a concentrated alkali every time he had a painful attack. During the consultation he could trace most of the attacks to a state of anxiety which he had lived with all his life. The lining of his stomach had become so severely inflamed that certain foods, or even overeating, could also bring on an attack. He had a problem in the solar plexus chakra which had originated in unhappy childhood experiences. Now the physical symptoms were warning him that the blockage had to be cleared before he grew any older or he risked even greater damage to his stomach and duodenum. It was explained to him that medical treatment alone might relieve the symptoms but this would be temporary. In time they would return because the energy blockage had not been released.

Robert required healing on many levels. Part of the healing involved helping him to understand the power of his own negative thoughts. He needed help emotionally and mentally to reprogramme his reactions to people and situations and to change his thought patterns. He was also recommended

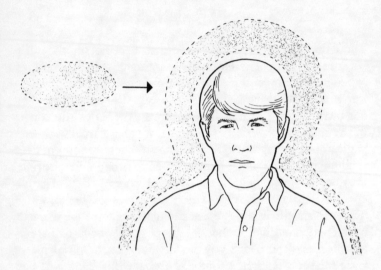

Fig. 11. How thoughts affect us: a negative thought form is attracted to a depressed person, impacting on his aura. Soon it will greatly increase the depression and negativity which is being experienced

to take a course of relaxation and stress management and a critical look at his eating habits.

Thoughts attract energies similar in structure to themselves so thought blocks are quickly built up. This can be useful when we need to tap into some knowledge, but devasting when we are in a negative state of mind as, periodically, was Robert. When we feel depressed our thoughts attract similar patterns of energy in the vicinity so that we may quickly find ourselves sinking deeper into negativity with all the miserable results which this can bring. On the other hand, if we exert our will in time to attract a positive thought block, it will immediately change the situation for the better.

The thoughts of others, if directed at us, will be received through the subtle energy system where they will have to be processed in the same way as our own thought energies. The implications for healing are that we can help ourselves and others by trying to keep our thoughts as positive as possible at all times – especially in negative situations or confrontations with other people.

Energy Imbalances

The two systems of the body – the physical and the etheric – are both essential to life and health. The ancient Indians and Chinese recognized these systems so that they still provide the foundations of their current medical practice. The flow of subtle energy between the two systems is the basis of acupuncture which is designed to remove energy blockages.

Spiritual healers have confirmed the findings of the Indians and the Chinese that the subtle or etheric system governs the physical system of the body. Disease and illness are the manifestations of energy imbalance or 'blockages' in the etheric system and physical symptoms can always be traced there. It follows that earlier diagnosis of the problem at the subtle level, followed by appropriate treatment, would restore the patient to health more rapidly.

A spiritual healer is able to help a patient towards this goal by detecting energy imbalances or blockages in the seven main chakras and in the secondary ones which are scattered around the body. Where this is the cause of the problem, healing acts first on the subtler levels of the body which, in turn, act on the physical. The picture is one of healing energies moving through the energy systems to remove blocks and restore balance. A feeling of good health is the physical sign that this has occurred.

The movement of sunlight through a droplet of water to produce the prismatic effect of the rainbow is explainable by the science of physics – yet it is still a source of joy and wonder. We know it is the manifestation of the movement of certain energies but the beauty of the event transcends mere knowledge. The human energy field, in terms of physics, is a series of events. But it is also a creation of wonder – the physical arena for the human spirit. The rainbow tells us about light and about water. The rainbow within the HEF conveys a message from our spiritual to our physical self.

Our health encapsulates this message, for our state of health is a clear expression of how we are processing different energies. It is a function of spiritual healing to inform us about this and the act of healing is a loving demonstration of this function.

4

What It Means to be a Healer

I T IS SAID that all of us are capable of healing and probably 90 per cent of those who attempt to channel healing energies are, to some degree, successful. But not all people wish to be part of that 90 per cent. Spiritual healing demands more than a well-meaning interest in other people's health. It demands a concern for the suffering of others which will motivate a person to offer them help. And the offer must be open day after day, week after week, year after year. This is the kind of staying power which will overcome the problems and difficulties that come a healer's way. Apart from this he must be prepared to make the effort to develop as a person as well as a healer.

Such are the personal qualities which will be needed to turn an ability into the highest craftsmanship and professionalism. They are essential if healing is to be a service to the community and an enhancement of that community.

The decision to become a healer, whatever else he pursues, is an important event in a person's life. Whether he realizes it or not, a new lifestyle has been entered into, new commitments made and new responsibilities taken on. An outline of these commitments and responsibilities, personal and public, form the basis of this chapter.

CHILD HEALERS AND SENSITIVITY

Many healers recall wanting to help those in distress from a very young age. Some even gave them assistance. Research in the USA has shown that it is quite common for healers to start exercising their gift from babyhood. A baby is simply a spirit in a tiny body which in no way diminishes his abilities as far as healing is concerned.

A mother in the USA, doing research on young children, tells how her baby daughter demonstrated an unselfish wish to heal other babies.[4] At the time she had given birth to a daughter who needed intensive care. The little girl began to improve and then suddenly became critically ill. After two days another baby in the unit died and her daughter began improving again. A few weeks later the baby relapsed. As the mother was cuddling her sick daughter one day she overheard nurses discussing another baby in the unit who was dying. Suddenly she realized that her own daughter had been picking up the conditions of the others. She quickly explained to her baby that she was not yet strong enough to look after her own body and help the other babies at the same time. This should be left to her own spirit helpers and her higher self who would give the required help. Straightaway her little daughter improved and soon became well enough to leave the hospital.

Many healing spirits bring with them, at birth, highly sophisticated knowledge which may be far in advance of any training courses which are currently on offer. For this reason, a healer's competence does not directly relate to his age, how long he may have been practising or what training he has undergone. As we move closer to the New Age it will become daily more evident that many thousands of highly evolved beings have been born recently, and are still being born, whose mission is to help humanity and the planet.

So the desire to reach out to help another is inborn and may show itself from the moment of birth. Along with such a desire, the infant healer may often exhibit other forms of heightened sensitivity. Some of these are the high sense perceptions of seeing, hearing and feeling which account for the child's psychic experiences. Others show themselves as childhood illnesses which have been empathetically taken on from a friend or relation.

Children who are naturally empathetic take on the pains and illnesses of those around them. This accounts for the 'mystery illnesses' developed by so many children. They are taken to the doctor who cannot find anything physically wrong. But a check on the health of their friends often reveals the cause of the condition. The doctor's diagnostic problem can be further compounded by the child who not only empathizes with another child but actually takes the condition away from them to bear it himself.

The sensitivity of a child healer will show itself in many ways as he grows up. It may often make life difficult for himself and those around him. The child may seem oversensitive at times, reacting to situations very strongly. This is because everything in life is deeply felt by such children. A thoughtless remark, violence or cruelty in any form, even if this is just seen on television, leave a mark on the sensitive child.

But sensitivity is one of the healer's greatest gifts for it actually enhances the healer's capacity to channel. Once the emotions are brought under control, the ability to absorb energies so easily is focussed on the act of healing. Sensitivity brings a greater ability to empathize with a patient's condition, both psychologically and physically. Thus parents and teachers of such children can do much to help them try to balance their feelings and learn the self-discipline which will be so essential in later life.

Children may show an aptitude for healing by the way they wish to help animals or plants as well as people. Encouraging and supporting concern for wildlife and the planet is an excellent way of channelling these positive energies.

Some cultures have a tradition of creating an environment where healing talents may be fostered from a very young age. From ancient times in Hawaii, for example, there have been a number of training schools devoted to different arts, including healing. Thorough training begins in childhood and those who master their art are called *kahuna*. This accords with the ancient cultures of Egypt, India and Greece where similar training was offered to children. Many Native American groups were also a foremost example of this type of nurture which is now beginning to see a welcome renaissance.

TRAINING

It is not part of our tradition to help child healers develop their gift and so it often remains dormant until later in life when some event brings it to the surface again. Though it may seem to remain dormant it is highly probable that the budding healer not only works on subtle levels but trains at these levels too.

Healers have been trained before they decide to incarnate on the Earth plane. Their training also continues during the sleep state when they can leave their bodies, as we all do, to attend special sessions on other levels. Many healers actually leave their bodies in the sleep state to continue their work with patients. Sometimes patients 'visit' a healer for the same reason. These phenomena are quite common and add a fascinating dimension to distant healing.

During a healer's career he may work with a guide for many years and then be passed on to another when a certain level of knowledge has been reached. Some healers say they have known their guide for many lifetimes. This close relationship of pupil with teacher means that the healer is constantly learning. He is able to pursue knowledge which is as yet quite unavailable in our colleges and universities.

These things may be true for a healer's inner experience, but his proficiency can only be demonstrated by the way he deals with his patients. The outside world needs assurances and, as with all forms of therapy, the public needs to be safeguarded. To this end the healing organizations were formed and, more recently, the Confederation of Healing Organizations.

Most healers are members of a recognized healing body which protects both themselves and their patients. The healer is insured and the patient can be guaranteed an approved level of competence. To become a registered Healer Member, he will have to provide evidence of apprenticeship and proficiency. In the UK, the healing organizations run training courses for probationer healers. Those of the National Federation of Spiritual Healers, especially, provide a broad and balanced curriculum with a high standard of excellence. Useful elements within such training courses include anatomy, physiology and first aid as well as a thorough study of the human energy field. Instruction and guidance is by practising healers and the probationer is further supported, in the case of the NFSH, by a national network of regional committees and the staff of community healing centres.

Part of the apprenticeship is to work alongside experienced healers. The apprentice takes part in healing sessions under supervision and is able to discuss his work with those who are providing the training. This is often at a healing centre or clinic where a number of healers are working together. A second method is to work with a healer as part of his healing practice. Training through the recognized bodies also ensures that the new healer is fully conversant with the legal aspects of healing and the code of conduct which is expected of him as a professional (see Chapter I).

Every healer needs guidance in the early stages and the help of someone who can answer questions and share experiences. But, ultimately, true guidance and authority come from the Source of healing energy itself. This is why the healer's own link with his higher self is so important. Practising the gift and taking time out for meditation or quiet moments away from all distractions are the best ways to forge this link.

Recognizing Healing Ability

Before a person decides to join a group or healing organization he may need confirmation that he has the ability to heal. Many people are reluctant to approach a healing group in case they find out that they are wrong. But the desire to use the gift for the benefit of others is a sign that it might well be a dormant talent. A common indicator is being singled out by other people as a listening ear. They seem instinctively to know that the person they are drawn to can help them in some way. Of course, this is often the operation of their own HSP! Sometimes, someone may even ask the budding healer if he will put his hands on them to relieve something like a headache or back ache. It is always wise to wait to be asked to do this, rather than to force healing on someone. This allows the higher self to operate rather than the ego – which may be looking for a pat on the back! A visit to a competent healer will soon clear up any doubts about healing ability one way or the other (see Chapter 7).

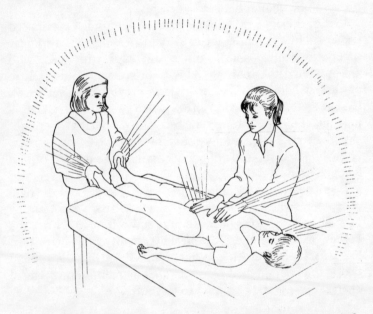

Fig. 12. While the healer works on the patient's solar plexus and sacral chakras, an apprentice healer is balancing the patient's energy field by directing energy via the feet. Healing energies, but not spirit helpers, are shown.

In public healing demonstrations people have been asked by the healer if they would like to participate, only to find that they

can feel healing energies flowing through them. In these cases
the healer has generally sensed that there are members of the audience who need the encouragement to get started and that it is
the right time for this to happen. Very often the catalyst is an
actual visit to a healer. During the course of treatment, many
patients feel tingling sensations or other feelings in the hands
which are often a clue to their own healing abilities.

Case History: Rose had been accompanying her young
husband at healing sessions for lesions he had received in
a car accident. One day she told the healer that her hands
always felt incredibly hot during her husband's treatment.
She had only to think about healing for her hands to break
out in a sweat and she was thinking of asking her doctor
about the problem. The healer suggested that she stay still
and send the energy out to her husband or to anyone else
who needed help. As soon as she did so her hands cooled
down.

It was pointed out to her that she was a channel for
healing energy and that in future she should help her
husband whenever he needed it. Rose was surprised and
delighted. She had often felt the urge to help other people
in pain but had never known what to do. The treatment of
her husband's condition had triggered off the gift which had
always been with her.

Sensitivity, Awareness and Responsibility

The healer's heightened awareness, which showed itself as
sensitivity in childhood, gives him the ability to appraise
another person. He can take into account their character
when assessing their needs and can distinguish the facts of
a situation from the fiction. But sensitivity brings advantages
and disadvantages of which the healer must be aware. If a
healer spends every day with sick people, absorbing their
conditions and problems, he would be seriously depleted by
the end of a week – if not already hospitalized! So he has to
know how to be sensitive on the one hand and how to protect
himself from the effects of negative energies on the other.

This requires practice and experience. It is one of the reasons why healers wash their hands, either physically with water or mentally, after attending to each patient. This breaks the link with the last patient so that a fresh one can be made with the next. Secondly, it ensures that nothing in the energy field of the previous patient is transferred to that of the next patient or himself. This routine is part of the healer's responsibility to himself and to his patients. It does not break the link between the Source of healing energies and the patient, or between healing entities and the patient.

Because a healer has these responsibilities, he must carry out the clearing and protecting routines, mentioned in Chapter 3, at the close of every day. If he forgets that he is a channel or instrument for healing, energies can easily be transmitted to the patient from his own energy centres instead of from the universal energy field. When this situation is allowed to occur on a regular basis, the initial energy depletion will be followed by a strain on the physical organs concerned.

At a seminar in London in March 1990, Dr Hiroshi Motoyama talked about his research with healers. He warned that overuse of any chakra will cause imbalance and disease. His research showed that in the case of the solar plexus, for example, psychic diagnosis could strain this centre, leading to digestive problems. He also found that heart disease, caused by the straining of the heart centre, was a result of the direct transmittance of energy and not the channelling of it. Dr Motoyama's research indicates how much healers need to be particularly careful to be attuned on every level before commencing healing and throughout any healing session.

During a lecture on healing, the speaker told her audience: 'There's always the same person at the top of my healing list – me!' The audience laughed. The healer explained that this was not her selfishness. 'If I'm sick, I won't be able to work for you, will I?'

This was her lighthearted way of telling her audience about some of the factors which healers need to be aware of if they are to function efficiently. And, as she pointed out, awareness only comes with training and experience.

Developing Unconditional Love

When a person makes the decision to be a healer, even if this only takes up a small part of his working day, he puts a particular pressure on himself. This is the pressure to overcome personal blocks and imbalances so as to allow his own energy system to function at a high level of efficiency.

Deciding to become a healer does not make a person healthy, balanced and whole overnight. But awareness of personal deficiencies is heightened along with a sense of responsibility to take action to bring about harmony, both in health and in lifestyle. A healer is someone other people will come to trust and rely on so that a firm foundation is essential.

Problems, sometimes buried deep in the subconscious, are brought to the surface to be dealt with. This is because the decision to heal is part of the healer's evolution as a person. Forces are attracted which create testing life situations. These are valuable experiences which tell the healer much about himself as a person. They also help to build a personality and character which can cope with any problem that a patient may bring – and some may be very challenging indeed.

The healer opens the healing channel through attunement. This is greatly enhanced by disciplines such as regular meditation and distant healing sessions. Attunement opens the way for unconditional love. The internationally known healer, Dennis Barrett, once remarked: 'Healing is all about love. You can't heal if you don't like people.'

He was referring to the force which makes the links in the healing triangle, between healer, patient and the Source. It is the force which links the healer to his own higher self and that of the patient's and the energy which creates the conditions that enable healing entities to work.

Unconditional love helps the healer to stand back and treat all patients with impartiality. It gives respect for a patient's integrity and dignity and demands the same confidentiality expected from a doctor or any other therapist. It ensures that he will do his best, irrespective of the condition, sex, race, colour, religion, sexual habits, social status or age of the person seeking help.

THE PARADOX OF PAIN

When a healer first begins working an improvement in the patient's condition, or better still a cure, is the welcome sign which confirms his abilities. Then more difficult cases present themselves with greater possibility of failure. On these occasions being able to draw on the experience of other healers is so useful. In all therapy, including orthodox medicine, 'no cure equals failure' is not the correct equation – for the reasons discussed in Chapter 2. A healer works with a patient, not the condition. The condition draws the attention of the patient to his needs so it is with these needs that the healer has to be concerned. This will lead to the true cure, whatever that might be.

Experience teaches that, in spite of all the suffering and difficulty which all of us have to go through in life, everything *is* all right. This is perhaps a paradox for any patient. How can a state of pain or distress be all right? The answer is that pain is the alarm bell which tells us either that something is wrong physically, emotionally or mentally, or that there is an imbalance or blockage in the subtle energy system – or that both levels are affected. Without the alarm bell we would not know. This is the vital function of pain. The experience of pain forces us to address a situation and it won't go away until we do. If the experience of pain and how we deal with it brings about some new understanding or insight then it has been invaluable to our development as people.

In this sense, everything is as it should be because everything is a learning situation for someone. If every problem and difficulty in our lives were removed we could not progress. Indeed, if there were no problems to overcome we would not choose to be born on the Earth plane at all.

The paradox of pain is part of a healer's life too. Every

healer has experienced some form of acute suffering at some time in his life. Hindsight gives each experience of suffering a value which it may not have appeared to have at the time. For it has not only helped the healer in his own life's journey but brought him closer to those whom he wishes to help. It is fine to sympathize with someone, but understanding born of real experience has far more to offer. To be a healer means to be entirely human. Human beings have their feet on the ground and their heads in the air. Our feet on the ground reminds us of physical reality and the planet, our reasons for coming here and our debt to the earth which gave us our physical body. Our head in the air reminds us of our spiritual reality and the other equally important levels of our being.

To be human means to integrate these two realities, allowing the spirit to shine through and light up life. A healer demonstrates how to do this every time he allows healing energies to flow through him – for this is what it means to be a healer.

5

The Range of Healing

Hᴇᴀʟɪɴɢ always works with energies so that it is just as possible to heal a situation as it is a body, a mind or emotions. The range of healing can be extended, therefore, according to the concerns and abilities of the healer. It could be said that wherever a healer wishes to apply his 'therapeutic touch' healing will be poured into that life or situation.

The placing of the healer's hands on, or near, the body may tell the patient that therapeutic activity has begun – and some patients need this reassurance – but since the energy links of love are set up by the mind, healing actually begins the moment the healing triangle is formed. Therefore it is perfectly possible for healing to be carried out without the patient seeing a healer at all, as long as some contact with the healer is made. This can happen during a telephone call, by letter or even by tape recording.

DISTANT HEALING

Distant healing (also known as absent healing) is an operation of the healer's mind which is used to set up the energy links in the same way as hands-on healing. As with contact healing, feedback is essential to maintain the link and to let the healer know what is going on. Healers receive numerous requests for distant healing every week so that the number of patients needing help continues to grow. It is necessary, therefore, for the healer to be told when someone can be removed from the healing list.

The late Harry Edwards affirmed that his distant healing work was as important as his hands-on sessions. Over the years many thousands of letters were put on file which testify to the efficacy of this aspect of his work. This service is now being carried on by the staff of the Harry Edwards Healing Sanctuary at Burrows Lea (see under addresses in Chapter 7). Most healers would agree that they experience the same degree of success with distant healing as they do with contact healing.

Distant healing usually involves a combination of forces acting in unison. When, however, it is carried out by the use of the healer's mind alone, it is a form of mental healing. This is the mental direction of healing energies by the healer to the patient – the healer is not calling upon or using forces outside himself.

Mental healing demands a healer who has the knowledge and ability to operate in this way. He must be able to understand exactly what energies the patient requires as well as how to control and direct them.

It is difficult to draw a line between the different forms of these healing activities. Some distant healing is in the form of a prayer or thought form which the healer sends out on the patient's behalf. Here, there is less mental control over the healing process which has been handed over to other healing forces. It will be appreciated that the mind is all-important in extending the range of healing, in identifying where help is required and in initiating the appropriate healing action.

HEALING AND THE ENVIRONMENT

As explained in Chapter 2, it is quite normal for healers to work with other healing entities so that the range of healing resources is greatly extended. This allows those healers who specialize in animals, for example, to work with healing entities who are, in turn, specialists in those fields.

Many writers have described the entities who work alongside plants and environmental forces to facilitate their growth and evolution.[5] These forces were contacted by many ancient societies. The seers of India saw them as beings of light which they called *deva* (Sanskrit: angel). These entities also include the nature spirits and elementals, all of whom live here with us. They are visible to HSP either as radiant creatures of all sizes or as figures which have been pictured as gnomes, elves, and so on.

Through writers such as Dorothy Maclean, these beings have been trying to help us understand the problems of the plant and mineral kingdoms and how they relate to the problems of the environment. There is a vast field of work here for the interested healer – the healing of the environment.

Of course it is not necessary for a healer to be able to commune with nature spirits to do this kind of work. The desire to help is paramount. Many healers have been working on behalf of the planet for some time, knowing that a landscape suffers as a person does, from damage to its energy systems. As knowledge and awareness increases more are joining them to devote their healing to environmental concerns.

THE HEALING ENERGY OF PLANTS

Plants have shown a great willingness and ability to cooperate with human beings in enhancing their life on Earth. Plants provide us with a convenient source of solar energy and food and it is thought that there is a herb which can deal with every human disease.

The efforts of herbalists have been extended into the fields of homoeopathy and spiritual healing by great researchers such as Dr Edward Bach. Using HSP, Dr Bach was able to communicate with plant entities to discover a form of homoeopathic treatment derived from the essences of plant flowers. The Bach Flower Remedies act on the subtle levels, particularly influencing feelings and attitudes. Their gentle action makes them an ideal complementary remedy which can be taken in conjunction with spiritual healing. In countries around the world the range of flower essences has been considerably extended and much more remains to be done in cooperating with plants to widen the scope of spiritual healing.

We seek the colours of nature when we want to relax or recharge our batteries. Out in the country, beneath the blue sky is the soothing green of the hills, trees and the wild plants of the wayside.

Many healers have been surprised at the unexpected way in which plants have found a place in their healing work. Then, on reflection, the arrival of plants and flowers in the visions and meditations of their patients has seemed so obviously relevant.

Case History: Sarah. After the breakup of her marriage, Sarah suffered weeks of anger and sadness and she began to feel that her divorce was a signal that she had failed as a woman. A friend told her about spiritual healing and wondered if it could help her overcome her terrible bouts of depression and feelings of worthlessness. Reluctantly, Sarah went to see a healer. At the first session the healer noticed her agitated state of mind and asked her to sit down while he tried to relax her. She described how, as his hands were lowered gently on her shoulders, she felt a rush of warmth and tenderness which made her want to cry.

The healer asked her if she could see anything with her inner vision. She could clearly see a garden. He asked her to find a seat in the garden and sit down. When she was comfortable he asked her what she could see around her. She was aware of three flowers – a large yellow tulip, a marigold and a red rose. The healer asked her to approach the flowers one by one. First she went over to the rose. She was aware of its deep rose-red colour. 'Breathe in the colour of the rose,' said the healer. She did so and went on to the marigold and the tulip in turn. Each time she had to breathe in the colour of the flower. Finally she was asked to thank the garden for what it had given her and slowly walk away from it until she felt herself back in the treatment chair.

Sarah sat quite still for a moment and then opened her eyes. Her face was calm and clear and the troubled expression which had tightened her features earlier had slipped away. As she sat breathing slowly and quietly the healer explained how the colours of the flowers she had seen in the garden had been exactly the right colours which she needed for her own healing. They had been used to balance her three lower energy centres which had been affected by the feelings she had imposed on herself as a result of her broken marriage and divorce.

Sarah then disclosed that she was a keen gardener and lover of plants but she had no idea that they could help her in this way. During the course of her treatments she saw a number of plants and birds which all contributed their energies in the form of different colours.

COLOUR AND HEALING

Some patients describe how they can see colours around them during healing. They are seeing the different frequencies of the healing energies as they are being directed to the energy centres or to parts of the physical body. Sometimes bands of colour are seen to encircle the patient and revolve around them like an electric coil around a magnet. Most healers and patients with developed HSP state that no two healings seem to be the same and that the patterns of energy being used each time (which can be identified as colour) change as the condition changes.

When energy levels are low, the body takes longer to recover so that a particular colour is frequently used to give the patient an energy boost. This is very much like putting the jump leads onto a car battery. Once the body has been given a sufficient input of energy it can cease drawing on the vital reserves which it had been using for survival. Energy can then be focussed on regaining health and strength.

The correct energy frequency carries out the healing work and colour acts as its facilitator. Colour occurs on all levels and is not a phenomenon of the physical spectrum alone. To those with developed HSP, the range of visible colours expands as the frequency of each level accelerates. Colours also appear to be clearer and more vibrant.

When energy is used to protect the patient or to enclose him in a healing 'envelope', again it is seen as colour. This occurs during treatment and afterwards when the patient needs to be protected until the next session. A single colour or bands of colour may be used. Sometimes the protective energy appears to be golden, capable of reflecting back energies that could undermine the patient while he is undergoing healing. On the etheric level, gold is a colour and not the effect of light on a certain metal. Silver is another pure etheric colour which, as well as being a protective colour, is often used to clear certain vibrations from a patient's energy field. Many colours can be used in this way when directed by the mind to do so.

Some healers are gifted with the ability to see and apply colours directly to a patient's condition. Lily Cornford[6] has been practising spiritual healing in this way for many, many years. She uses, for example, a particular spring green to clear an organ of toxins, rose-pink to uplift the spirits and violet to heal the heart. Knowing that the shade and vibrancy of a colour are important, she teaches her students by referring to the flowers which may exhibit them, such as a daffodil, rose or delphinium. One of her many outstanding successes is the case of Jamie, a six-year-old boy with leukodystrophy. At eighteen months of age he had been given only six months to live, with the expectation of progressive mental and physical deterioration. With Lily's treatment he is now one of the brightest boys in his class and expects to walk without the aid of crutches.

Interpreting colour in the chakras

The qualities that are inherent in any energy are very often only visible through the results of their application. But when energies, like healing energies, have colour, the fact that they can be seen makes their study much more accessible. This study is extending the boundaries of possibility within healing, for each rainbow of colour supplies clues to the complex series of human energy patterns.

Colour is the clue to the state of a person's energy field and the interpretation of colour in the HEF is an important aspect of spiritual healing. As described in Chapter 3, each energy centre has a colour which also extends to the relevant area of the physical body. When healer and patient work together to discover what energies are operating in the chakras, they are revealed through colour.

For example, if a patient could not see the colour yellow in his inner vision, when working in this way, there might be a blockage in the solar plexus centre. When directed to this centre during the healing session, the patient might then see other colours or a yellow contaminated in some way. By combining the information given by all the chakras, the healer receives an overall picture of the patient's condition on the level of his energy centres.

Case History: Tom was a highly intelligent eleven-year-old boy who was taken by his mother for healing because of his regular bedwetting. The healer did not usually take her child patients through their chakras but in this case decided to do so. Tom could see a clear bright pink but could not link this colour to any part of his body. He saw a medium orange with blue and black round the edges which again he could not relate to any part of his body. Yellow was clear, a little dark with a smudge of black on it. Tom related this colour to his feet. The green he saw was cloudy and very dark. It did not relate to his body. He saw a blue which was darker than sky with white blotches on it. This colour he said was connected with his head. Indigo was also dark and Tom related the colour to his mind. He saw a medium colour of violet which was fairly clear and related to his eyes. Finally he was asked if he could see the colour white. This he saw as very bright and relating to his right hand.

Through her long experience in working with colour, the healer was able to draw a number of conclusions about Tom. He was certainly very intelligent though his school work might well be affected by the emotional problem which was linked to the bedwetting. This problem she thought was probably due to Tom's relationship with his father. His mind was troubled and this was further aggravating his sleep. The healer felt that Tom was also not happy about his feet in some way.

Tom's mother explained that, apart from wetting his bed, he also had regular nightmares. He went to bed very late and had his own TV in his bedroom. His parents allowed him to watch the late films, thinking it might help him to sleep. The healer pointed out that the late night television viewing was having the opposite effect because of its violent or disturbing content. She noted that Tom only wore one kind of footwear – trainers. These were made of synthetic materials which were making his feet hot and sweaty. There was soreness and broken skin between many of his toes.

Tom had been able to give a comprehensive picture of the state of his energy centres. He was seeing the energy around him as bright – normal for a young person. His inability, however, to relate deep pink to himself showed that he needed lots of love and affection. The impurities in the sacral (orange) chakra showed that the emotional problem visible in his solar plexus and heart would probably manifest as a physical symptom in the urogenital system – as indeed it did.

His higher centres gave encouraging clues that Tom would one day be able to use his mind and eyes for the benefit of others and he would certainly develop his powers of HSP.

Tom's first consultation is presented here to show that what is happening to a person physically, emotionally and mentally is visible at the level of the chakras. Such information is invaluable to the spiritual healer who can interpret it.

In little Tom's case the healer could see colour being used to clear and energize his chakras and the changes brought about were soon visible in his aura. Sometimes it is the direct application of colour to a person's aura which is most immediately needed.

Case History: Mike had been to a healer for treatment and mentioned a number of situations which he found stressful and probably contributory to his digestive problem. Interactions with certain people particularly worried him – his aggressive boss, tough negotiators on the telephone and, perhaps worst of all, Jim, a member of his sailing crew.

The healer advised him to 'think pink'. This meant visualizing the people he had mentioned surrounded by an aura of rose pink every time he thought of them or was due to encounter them. The healer explained that this was a key colour in the vitality energy which has a tremendously strengthening and soothing effect on the nervous system.

Mike was a little baffled by the idea but said he would try it after the healer had shown him that he could see the colour with his inner vision any time he liked. A few weeks later Mike was entered in an important yacht race. He was dreading the outcome if things did not go well; he had had enough of Jim's tantrums. But he had been 'surrounding him with pink' throughout the previous day. The weather became rough and they lost a few places. Mike braced himself for an outburst which never came. Instead, Jim spoke philosophically about the race and life in general and worked hard to keep the boat on course.

Mike told the healer how Jim's normal demeanour had totally changed. Through seeing the results, Mike learned an important lesson about the healing power of the mind which, in turn, helped him to overcome his own condition.

CLEARING NEGATIVE ENERGIES

When some healers are asked to apply their skills to clear negative energies from around people or out of buildings, they feel that this goes beyond the scope of healing. A contact, or hands-on, healer especially, may see no connection between healing patients and healing the effects of a negative influence.

Healers are caring, giving people but their right to give their time and energy in the way they see fit must be respected. So must their feelings about their own work. The range of a healer's work is not a comment about abilities or dedication, it simply defines their interests.

The day may come when a healer is asked to help with a situation such as 'possession', 'exorcism' or 'ghost busting'. He may feel that the case has been brought to his notice because he is the right person to deal with it – and this is usually so. In this way, many healers have found their work extended.

There is always a rational explanation for 'supernatural' events. Healers have to work within natural law in all cases and they have found that there is nothing which is outside the law. People may be subjected to negative energies for a number of reasons. They may have deliberately opened themselves energetically and psychologically as occurs during seances or using ouija boards.

When people do these things they are generally unsupervised and ignorant of what is happening. Human beings have free will and when we decide to dabble in the occult our guardian angel must stand back, powerless to stop us. We will have to learn by what transpires. Such dabbling is an invitation to mischief-making entities to draw near to people and cause all kinds of trouble.

Healers who can deal with these problems have the strength of character, spiritual development and mind power which allows no fear or prejudice to take over. They are confident in their own abilities to clear negative energies, either by themselves or with the help of healing guides and helpers.

But the practice of black magic (the use of subtle energy in a totally negative and destructive way) or Satanism goes further than mere dabbling. Here people have made a conscious decision to manipulate energy to harm and destroy. Their deliberate denial of the Source and function of energy will eventually have catastrophic effects on the practitioners. This is due to the law of cause and effect which is part of natural law. All energy that we send out will eventually return to us. As it moves through the universal energy field it attracts similar energy to itself so that it has a far greater force when it finally returns to the generator.

The darkness that is built up through black magic requires an equal and opposite force to disperse it and neutralize it, especially from the minds of its practitioners or those close to such people. For the power of evil radiates outwards, according to the force put into it, to affect the people and places near to it. A healer's knowledge and conviction that darkness is the absence of light and that light always overcomes darkness, gives him the confidence to work even in these unhealthy areas. But they are no place for the fainthearted!

Energy generated by people in a place outdoors or in the rooms of buildings is absorbed by that place or rooms. These energy traces are virtually indestructible, unless cleared by someone with the mental ability, and can therefore last for centuries. This is why some healers and those with developed HSP can 'pick up' the energies left at the scene of a crime or some evil happening, whenever this might have occurred. The place needs to be healed because the negative power of the stored energies can affect anyone who comes within their range. This phenomenon accounts for most cases of what is known as 'exorcism'. It is rare that an evil spirit inhabits a place; the evil is far more likely to be the effects of the horrible actions of men and women.[7]

Any negative thought or action drags down the whole of creation, just as positive thoughts and actions elevate it. We are living in a time when the negative aspect of existence, which has unbalanced human life, is being drawn to the surface and exposed for us to see. This is not to make human life more unbearable but to allow us to bring about the balance which we and the planet need to move on to the next stage of our evolution. Evil can be dealt with more easily when it can be seen and light always causes the darkness to shrink. This is where healing thoughts and actions come in.

Patients sometimes go to see a healer with a complaint which has baffled their doctor. If the healer is able to see the patient's aura a common and insidious cause of the condition is often revealed – the energy traces of the negative thoughts of another. When thoughts of anger, dislike or hatred are consistently focused on another person, that person may be seriously affected – for these are energies with an accumulative power to harm, injure or even destroy.

When such a cause is revealed, the patient is treated for the condition in the usual way as well as being taught how to protect himself against the force being directed at him. The patient may also need counselling to expose and get rid of a destructive relationship or to break the link with someone who wishes him ill.

HELPING DISTRESSED SPIRITS

A source of energy around a person which is not negative, but which could be troubling him, is that of one who has passed over. For a variety of reasons, people return to this plane to draw close to someone. It could be a strong bond of love and the entity simply wishes to let the person know that it is there or wants to help him. Sometimes spirits stay in a place to warn the other occupants of a danger which is still present there.

Cases are also recorded where people have passed over in great distress or in an accident and are not conscious of having left their physical bodies. They feel that something is still unresolved in their life so they stay around the place which is the focus of their unhappiness. Anyone who is slightly psychic will sense the presence of such distraught people and of course be highly disturbed by it.

A healer does not have to be clairvoyant to be able to help in these situations, though it is an advantage. He can mentally communicate with the distressed person to explain what has happened and that they need to move away from the physical plane and go towards the light so that they can carry on with their lives. People are never left to do this alone. Loving entities step forward to comfort them and show them the way.

Conditions are created through the agency of the healer for spiritual forces to operate and heal the situation. Sometimes there are unforeseen but promising outcomes to these healings.

Case History: A suicide. A clairvoyant healer was contacted by a couple who were setting up a small therapeutic home for children. They did not know when they bought the house that a former occupant had committed suicide there, but the wife had felt uncomfortable in many of the rooms from the day they moved in. The healer agreed to visit the house to see what was wrong.

As she stood in the front room she became aware of a very distressed entity – the man who had committed suicide. He told her that he had been a teacher but the problems in his private life had overcome him and driven him to take his life. The healer had to fight back her own tears for it was obvious that the teacher was still suffering some of the emotional turmoil of that time. She told him that the couple had no fear of him and that he was welcome to come to the house as long as he caused no trouble. The couple asked the healer if she would tell him about their proposed work with children. The teacher said he wanted to help and the healer told him that this would be welcomed too. He said he would come to the house to try to learn as well as to help and he was led away crying, but this time his tears were of joy.

The couple felt that the healer had healed the situation in an extremely positive way through her loving response to all those concerned.

CONFLICT AND PEACE

In terms of energy, the changing of vibrations to repair that which is damaged is a healing act which brings back balance and harmony. Many healing groups are now directing their distant healing meetings to the healing of situations. The healing triangle is created except that this time the 'patient' is perhaps a community in trouble or distress, a situation of conflict or an environmental problem of some kind. The group do not assume that they know what is the right or best outcome but instead they project the energy of love into the situation and let it do its healing work. This is a form of distant healing or prayer which can be practised by anyone who is disturbed by reports on the television, radio or in the newspapers.

Peace on earth depends on the peace within our hearts and minds. Because of the laws that govern the effects of energy, balance and harmony have to begin with ourselves. There can be no peace out there if there is a state of conflict within. Healing works on our energies to change the state of conflict to one of harmony by its effect on all levels of our being.

By confronting the problems which reflect a universal need for healing, spiritual healers are reaching out to heal the whole of life.

6

Healing and the Cycle of Life

REINCARNATION

B ECAUSE LIFE is a continuous state, we have all lived before
coming to this planet and we will carry on living after leaving
our bodies here. We have to accept that we have incarnated
here, but for many the idea that we may have reincarnated is
more difficult to accept. Healers may never have to confront
their own beliefs or feelings on the subject since it is a fact that,
whether or not they accept the concept of reincarnation, this
has no bearing on their ability to channel healing energies.

But there are occasions which challenge the healer's belief.
The healing entities or spirit helpers who work with him tell
him about their previous lives on Earth, sometimes assuring
him that the healing partnership has grown stronger over many
lifetimes. Or the day may come when he has to deal with the
effects of incidents which seem to have taken place in the past
life or lives of a patient.

The healer has the option to accept the patient's account
of past-life trauma as part of his condition and treat it in
the usual way. Or he can accept that the trauma did
occur in previous lives, the memories were lodged in the
subconscious, and the patient is still suffering the effects of
them because they have not been healed. Whichever option
he chooses, the correct energies will still be channelled to the
patient.

The final healing may, however, depend on the patient's understanding of why he has been suffering. He may want to know how incidents which had never occurred in his life nevertheless appear so vividly in his mind. Through the course of the treatment he can be confident that he will be shown how this occurs and how unpleasant memories may be healed.

There are now well-documented cases of children recalling past lives. American research indicates that they start talking about their past lives around the age of three but have usually forgotten these experiences by the age of eleven.[8]

A BBC TV programme ('40 Minutes', March 1990) showed the case of a young Indian boy who could describe how he had been murdered in a previous lifetime, a killing which had been well recorded at the time. He could remember where and when the shooting took place and, most strikingly, he had a mark on his head in exactly the same place where the bullet had entered the murdered man's skull. Dr Satwant Pasricha of the National Institute of Mental Health and Neurosciences in Bangalore had studied 250 such cases of reincarnation. In over a quarter, subjects exhibited physical marks or phobias connected with their previous lives.

Furthermore, the boy could remember incidents and places from his previous life which could all be corroborated. Perhaps the most bizarre aspect of the case was the fact that his wife (in the former life) was still alive. A visit to her and the young boy's descriptions of intimate moments in their married life convinced her that he was indeed her former husband!

Children's dreams also reveal vivid descriptions of other times which they could not have learned about. Some of them even concern the decision to be reborn on the Earth plane and the preparations which had to be made for this to take place.

THE SOUL'S JOURNEY

The whole question of our decision to be born, where and when and to which parents, has great importance in healing.

Healers are confronted not only with the illnesses of children but also their deaths and the need to comfort the grieving parents. It is helpful for parents to realize that the child does indeed choose its parents. It is a spirit in its own right with a destiny which may not necessarily conform with the wishes of its parents.

It is sometimes very hard for a healer to explain these aspects of life to people in distress, but healing is part of the whole life of spirit – not just the small span of time that may be spent on Earth. Healers find that viewing life from a physical point of view alone is a denial of our true nature and a stunting of human potential. So our life and our health have to be seen as part of an ongoing and developing journey of discovery. When people can cooperate with spirit and allow it to undertake its soul journey in its own way, especially when it is a child, much misunderstanding and unhappiness will be avoided.

Case History: John. When baby John was born with a severe heart defect the specialists told his parents that he would die within a few weeks unless a suitable heart could be found for a transplant operation. A member of the family asked for healing to be sent to the baby. On making a connection with little John, the healer realized that it was the baby's wish only to experience the time in his mother's womb and the process of birth. He would soon leave his body. Aware that such news would only distress the parents, the healer still asked for healing energy to be sent so that John could use it in whatever way he needed.

The baby was put on a life-support machine while a suitable heart donor was found. John now assured the healer that he had left his body and would do all he could to help his parents to come to terms with his passing. A donor was found and the transplant operation took place; this proved unsuccessful. Sadly, the healer was not in a position to comfort the parents with the truth that John had fulfilled his destiny and wanted to thank them for this.

Knowing that it will be some time before people accept and understand our spiritual nature, healers in such a dilemma can only promise to do what they can. Thoughts of love or healing are never wasted and the energy generated by them is always put to good use.

HEALING AND PREGNANCY

Some parents are able to accept the destinies of their sick children and welcome the support which healers can offer in such cases. Children respond well to healing and examples, such as that of Jamie, mentioned in Chapter 5, are common to most healers' files. Because the child is a spirit with few if any of the mental and emotional barriers which are present in the average adult, it can be contacted very easily. This is true even of a babe in the womb.

Case History: A Breech baby. A young woman approached a healer after a meeting of her local meditation group and asked if her sister could be helped by distant healing. Her sister was unmarried and pregnant. The baby was in the breech position and due quite shortly. Her sister had been told that she would have to have a Caesarian operation because, no matter how often her baby was turned, it would not stay in the correct position. There was a great deal of pressure on the sister to marry but she had no wish to do so. She was thus suffering from excessive stress and not looking forward to the birth of her child.

The young woman was told that healing would be sent to her sister and to let the healer know what occurred the following week. During the distant healing session, the healer could feel the baby being turned in the womb and received the assurance that all would be well and that the birth would be normal. The birth was now imminent and the healer asked the young woman to tell him how it went for her sister. Two weeks later, he met her again at the meditation group and she told him that her sister had not only produced a fine baby without an operation, but that it had been a very easy birth and the mother was looking radiant.

91

HIGHLY EVOLVED CHILDREN

We are living in a time when many highly evolved children are being born. In spiritual terms 'highly evolved' means of a high degree of understanding. These children are generally far in advance of their parents in their understanding of the world, human nature and spiritual realities. They possess a range of well-developed subtle energetic and spiritual abilities as well as physical ones, which will equip them to achieve the full potential of the New Age to which this planet is destined. It is part of their destiny not only to help and serve humanity but also the planet as an entity in its own right.

It has to be realized that these children have the veil of incarnation across their vision, as we all do. The world into which they have entered may seem bewildering, even terrifying. They need careful nurture in their early years to come to terms with being entrapped, as it were, in a tiny body. This acts as a severe limitation for an advanced soul until control and maturity have been developed.

Parents and teachers have identified some of these children as hyperactive or severely withdrawn. When they have been taken to a healer, however, light has immediately been thrown on their behaviour problems. Sometimes the parents are themselves psychically aware and are relieved to find that their assessment of the child as an advanced soul has been correct. In other cases the revelation has led to an opening up of parental interest in a range of subjects from astronomy to reincarnation.

Clairvoyant teachers have testified to startling telepathic communications with infants on a level far above their chronological age. Such teachers are able to encourage them to develop and use their gifts rather than to dismiss or ridicule them.

For those who have come into contact with these new souls, the future they present is indeed a thrilling one. They possess knowledge, or have access to knowledge, which is not yet understood by the best minds of their elders. It is up to those who are interested in the future to appreciate that a great healing is taking place on all levels. It has to take place so that these wonderful children can fulfil their mission to transform human life on Earth. This is why healing is so prominent and so widespread.

In terms of energy, what affects one affects us all. We all need healing so that together we can take the next step forward in our evolution. To do this the heart chakra has to be unblocked and unconditional love allowed to flow freely. On a planetary scale, this is a massive undertaking. But healing asks us to look closely at the latest health scourges for clues which are showing the way. Love and compassion have been mobilized many times on a global scale to feed the starving children of the Third World. Yet it is estimated that thousands of children continue to die every year.

THE CHALLENGE OF AIDS

Babies are now being born HIV positive and the number of children suffering from AIDS is growing rapidly. So far the global response has largely been one of revulsion or disbelief. As workers in the field, such as Dr Elisabeth Kübler-Ross, have pointed out, AIDS confronts us all with the two great taboos of sexuality and death. Added to this is the image of a baby born with HIV, a baby who still needs to be hugged and cared for. From a healer's point of view, AIDS is a challenge to human love, a chance to unblock the heart chakra of the human race. In this sense it is perhaps the ultimate challenge.

HEALING AND YOUNG PEOPLE

Teenagers and young people are frequent visitors to healing practices and many of them are seeking help with the everyday problems of growing up. Very often their problems are compounded by psychic occurrences which are considered distressing and seem to them to have no purpose. Healers can do a great deal to help young people come to terms with their latent abilities and to show them how they may play a natural, but not necessarily a prominent, part in their lives.

Case History: Mark. When Mark and his wife went for healing they both asked for help with depression. They had recently married and set up a hairdressing business at the same time. The healer started to work on the young man and was impressed with the feeling that Mark was not anxious about the business and that his marriage was working well. Something else was bothering him.

Mark agreed. He had been on a motorbike with his brother, Gwyn, when they were involved in a fatal accident. Gwyn was killed while Mark was thrown off the bike. Since the funeral, Mark had felt his brother tapping him on the shoulder. His wife said she had actually 'seen' him in the house and was very upset by this. They wanted an explanation and they wanted Mark's brother to leave them alone.

The healer was able to reassure them that Gwyn had simply been trying to make contact with them because he knew what they were going through and he wanted to show them that he was all right. They were sensing his presence because of their own natural sensitivity and psychic abilities. It was wonderful to know that Gwyn was trying to heal their unhappiness.

It was suggested to the couple that the next time they were aware of Gwyn they should thank him for coming, tell him they now understood and would be happy for him to get on with his new life. The healer also counselled Mark that part of his depression was due to guilt that he had survived the accident and not his brother. But Gwyn understood his feelings and was adamant that Mark should throw away the guilt because now he was fine.

On their next visit to the healer, a few weeks later, it was obvious that the couple's depression had lifted. They had received another 'visit' from Gwyn and had talked to him. Since then he had not returned.

HEALING IN HOSPITAL

Even when the patient is in the hands of a doctor, or in hospital, healing can still be of great benefit. Though a hospital is intended to be a caring environment it is a traumatic experience for the patient, involving separation from loved ones, confinement and anxiety. Most hospitals welcome spiritual healers if they have been requested by a patient since healing can often provide the strength and reassurance needed to cope with the situation. Furthermore, help can be sent on a distant basis to both the patient and those who are working on his behalf – the doctors, surgeons, nurses, etc.

Sometimes the healer can encourage the patient in hospital to realize that the illness provides a time for inner contemplation or life assessment. Healing can also help a person to accept a condition which must be faced and to come to terms with it. This changes the period of ill health and confinement from a time in limbo to one of positive growth for the patient.

HEALING AND OLD AGE

Old age presents the healer with a range of problems since illness at this stage in life is so often due to the accumulation of events which have occurred over a long period of time. The effects of nutrition, traumatic experiences, lifestyle, habits of thinking, emotional reactions, loneliness, patterns of ill health, fear of death, are some of the pressures with which the older person must contend. This maze of forces will be unravelled in a way best suited to each individual.

A pattern which so often emerges, however, is one known to all who care for the elderly or the terminally ill – the need to complete unfinished business. During healing sessions patients express long-repressed feelings of anger, bitterness, shame and guilt. These feelings are frequently directed towards family members but they may also be strongly felt against those who have long passed over. They are, in effect, suffering from spiritual deprivation.

When a patient is prepared to accept this fact and wishes to do something about it, healing can mobilize powerful and constructive energies. Blockages can be worked on and unfinished business brought out into the open. A negative view of life, generated by a refusal to learn and grow from experience, has no value for the person holding it nor for those on whom they inflict it. But it is possible during healing meditations for patients to meet people and events from the past and to have their experiences healed.

It is never too late for these things to happen. Only the will on the part of the patient and healer to allow them is needed. This sets in motion the healing process which will gently take the patient where he needs to go. Thus elderly people are guided to see that there is a purpose to their lives and that each day is meaningful.

Old age is a time for contemplation and consolidation when, through the application of love, experience may become wisdom. Wisdom has the power to heal and is the antidote to cynicism and bitterness.

A SPIRITUAL VIEW OF DEATH

For older people who have accepted healing in a relaxed manner, being prepared to go with the treatment, the fear of illness or death can be tackled. Healing offers a point of view of death which has developed from the practical experiences of working with patients and entities on higher frequencies of life. It is the point of view which is presented throughout this book.

In simple terms, death or passing over is the casting off of the physical body by the spirit who no longer needs it. This occurs when the life force ceases to flow into the physical body via the etheric body which is closest to it. The person gives up life in the physical body and moves on to the next stage of life in a subtler body which is far less limiting and in no way affected by damage or disease. This subtle body looks very much like the physical one to clairvoyant sight and is quite recognizable to those with developed HSP.

There is actually no death and that is why the term 'passing over' has more relevance. For the healer it is not a time of sadness or failure, far from it. Passing out of the physical enables the soul to take the next step on its journey.

The Near Death Experience

The Near Death Experience, or NDE, is a modern phenomenon which has come about through the ability to resuscitate people who have begun the process of dying. They have returned to physical life and have been able to report an experience (the NDE) which has come to be corroborated by world-wide research across many cultures and religions. The NDE is far more than the drowning person's past life rushing before his inner vision. Most common experiences are floating away from the body and moving down a brilliantly lit tunnel. As the subject moves into the light he is enveloped in a sense of utter peace and love. Relatives and friends come forward to welcome and reassure him. A shining being appears, to take him further. If resuscitation occurs the subject returns to his physical body.

Research by the doctor and scientist, Elisabeth Kübler-Ross, into 20,000 Near Death Experiences includes the accounts of blind people. They were able to describe clothes and colours worn by medical staff and the medical procedures taking place as they 'looked down' on themselves during the early stages of detachment from the body. The NDE research is a scientific endorsement of the experiences of healers who have been involved in helping the terminally ill.

Case History: Kenneth. A healer who had been working with a cancer patient for some weeks was called to his bedside at the local hospital. Kenneth had already told his relatives that he no longer had the resources to go on fighting and had had enough. The healer was clairvoyant and was able to see shining entities gather round his bed. Quietly Kenneth slipped away and the healer gently described to his family what was taking place. Kenneth sat up in his etheric body, smiling and looking round at them all. Then he stood up and thanked the healer for her help. The next moment he took the hands of the spirit helpers and left the room. He gave a message of hope and comfort to the family and promised that he would come back to see them soon. The family members were thrilled to hear this account which did much to help them bear the shock of his passing.

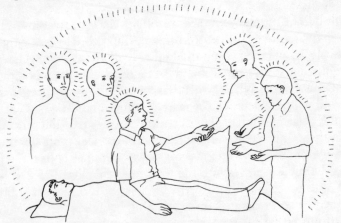

Fig. 13. Passing over: the patient, having just passed over, sits up in bed in his etheric body. Shining entities come forward to assist him. Spirit healers stand close by

Healing in Hospices

Some relatives tend to think of the hospice as the last port of call, a place which has no role for the spiritual healer. Yet this is where a great deal may still be done, both for the living and the dying.

Case History: Linda was an Italian Catholic whose mother, Maria, was dying of cancer. She practised her religion but felt that something was urging her to contact a healer on her mother's behalf. The healer arrived at the hospice to find a frightened middle-aged woman whose head had been shaved.

With a quavering voice she spoke in Italian and the healer answered as best he could. But the real communication took place without words.

First of all the healer had shown no shock at her appearance. He took her hand and placed his other hand between her shoulders where she complained of intense pain. In ten minutes she indicated that the pain had gone and she felt much calmer. Talking to her daughter outside, the healer was told that Maria was upset about her estranged husband. They had not met for years and she wanted to be reconciled with him before she passed over; she was battling to stay alive so that this could happen. So far, nothing could induce the husband to visit her, even though he lived near the hospice.

The healer promised he would do what he could and directed distant healing to the dying woman in the usual way. The following day the husband appeared unannounced at the hospice and had a long talk with Maria. The duty nurse said there were many tears followed by hugs and smiles. Later that night Maria passed away peacefully in her sleep.

The Power of Loving Thought

Part of a healer's role in preparing people for the experience of death may be his ability to explain many of the phenomena which occur around this time. Research in Australia shows that terminally ill patients may be prepared for death through dreams. Such patients frequently 'see' old friends or relatives who have passed over. They come to the bedside, talk to them and comfort them. Sometimes patients are shown glimpses of 'the other side', as in the NDE. Such things are perfectly normal and natural and any healer will be pleased to hear about them and discuss them if the patient so wishes.

We should all be assured that those who are passing will benefit from healing thoughts and prayers since they are in reality living souls who may well need that extra boost of energy to help them on their way. This is particularly the case where people have been suffering from a long-drawn-out or debilitating illness.

Case History: Bruce's father had been taken into a hospice suffering from the advanced stages of motor-neurone disease. Bruce was very upset about his father's condition but could think of no way to help him. Bruce's girlfriend, Rachel, did the only thing she could think of and telephoned a healer who had been recommended to them.

On hearing of the father's condition, the healer said that he would do what he could via distant healing. He explained that the father was a free spirit and would use the healing energy to do what he needed most. This might be to help him get better or it might just as well be to help him pass over. Whatever happened it could only benefit the patient if both she and Bruce sent their love to him.

Rachel listened carefully and the healer asked her if Bruce was ready to accept that his father might pass over. She said he was. The healer said he would send healing to both of them too.

An hour later, Rachel rang to say that Bruce's father had passed away round about the time they were talking on the telephone. The healer made a point of thanking her for her loving thoughts which had allowed higher forces to help the sick man and which would now serve to support them in their grief.

Relations should always remember that if their loved one has decided to pass over he can make valuable use of healing as well as loving thoughts. They should be careful not to let their own desire to keep the patient here on the Earth plane thwart that of the spirit who seeks release.

HEALING AND BEREAVEMENT

The funeral is rarely the end of a healer's work since support is still needed by the relatives and friends who have been left behind. The expression of grief is essential to the health of the bereaved. This is because powerful energies surge from the emotional centres in the body and the etheric body which need to be released. In some cultures it is considered unseemly for people to show their true feelings in public, especially if they are men. This is unfortunate since such energies, when not allowed to flow, naturally set up blockages which will eventually manifest as physical damage or disease. The most common place for grief blocks to occur is in the throat centre where the need for crying or shouting has been repressed. They may also show up in the solar plexus and heart chakras.

People who have passed over understand grief and it is quite normal for them to return to their loved ones to help and reassure them that all is well. It is thought that some 40 per cent of bereaved persons have sensed the presence of the relative or friend, to whom they were close, soon after the passing. This usually takes the form of 'seeing' them. Sometimes they are felt or even smelt! This happens when a spirit creates the familiar scent of tobacco, perfume, flowers, etc. to reassure the loved one that it is truly them. They come back to testify that there is no death but, sadly, so many feel they must be experiencing an hallucination due to the effects of grief.

Healers are always prepared to sit with the bereaved to initiate this process. For though a period of grief is essential to release the energies which have accumulated within, excessive grief is an unhealthy condition which requires help. It also creates a negative link with the one who has passed over which tends to draw them back to the physical level, preventing them from fully commencing the next stage of their life.

Case History: Dorothy and Malcolm. Dorothy had been grieving over the death of her teenage son, Malcolm, for over a year. He had died suddenly and unexpectedly at the age of eighteen, leaving a big gap in the family. His mother had been constantly aware of him from the time of the funeral, and so had his sister, but this only intensified their feelings of unhappiness. It seemed that everyone in the family was suffering from Malcolm's death and Dorothy was at her wit's end. Then she saw an advertisement from a local healing centre. She was reluctant to share her problem with anyone but that evening in desperation she found herself going to the centre for help. She saw a healer with an empty chair in front of him and sat down and blurted out her story.

As she spoke, the healer felt the presence of the deceased young man and was able to relay his conversation with Malcolm to his mother. Firstly, Malcolm gave his mother proof of who he was and then told her how he wanted everyone to stop grieving. There was a very strong bond of love between him and his mother which could not be broken even by death. Their relationship had now entered a new phase. Dorothy should accept that she was sensing his presence and could communicate with him.

During the healing session the healer worked on her heart and throat chakras. Afterwards he explained to Dorothy that she had to discover for herself how a relationship is perfectly possible between a soul on one frequency of life and that on another, once the 'lines of communication' had been opened. This was the exciting 'new phase' that Malcolm was talking about.

Dorothy was amazed and relieved by the healer's words which confirmed what she had already felt deep inside. Now she had an incentive to accept Malcolm's passing and look forward to developing the new relationship which he wanted her to make with him. Her acceptance not only improved her own health but that of the other family members who had been close to Malcolm.

Sometimes the healer's task in helping the bereaved is not as joyful when links with those who have passed over are negative ones. For example, there may have been no love lost and resentment still festers in the heart of the one left behind. Actual hatred may be the bond which holds two souls in an iron, suffocating grip.

Unhealthy links are forged by people who allow circumstances to create them. Petty disputes, divorce, abuse, violence, cruelty and even murder are the negative events whose energies are stored deep within a person's heart and mind. Healing can break these links if a person is ready and willing to rid themselves of the poisonous energies, to forgive where necessary and, most of all, to change. The wonderful thing about such healing is that it also benefits the one who has passed over and is thus an act of love in the highest sense.

We come to this planet because our higher self wishes to have an experience which only the Earth plane can provide. This is what makes the planet which has given us our physical bodies so unique and so special. We enter the world at the moment of birth and the cycle of our life here becomes part of Earth's being. The experience is a necessary part of our evolution – we cannot move on without it.

Healing shows us that our progress through the cycle of life is a chance to let the energy of love flow through us, to enrich and heal us; to let it flow out to enrich and heal all creation. For when we link, with love, to the light that is everywhere – healing must follow.

7

Taking It Further

THE LAST DECADE OF the twentieth century has seen a great increase in the number of trained subtle energy healers, and in the number of people seeking their help. Many parts of the world now look to developments in the UK for models of training, organization and practice. Trained healers belong to a professional healing organization. The Confederation of Healing Organizations (CHO) now comprise some fifteen member organizations, including the National Federation of Spiritual Healers (NFSH). The CHO, and the British Complementary Medicine Association (BCMA), are the umbrella bodies to which most healing organizations in the UK belong. They negotiate with orthodox medicine, government and the rest of the European Community. The aim of the two bodies is to see that subtle energy healing becomes a fully integrated part of health care provision in the UK and that training is of a high standard, with a professional code of conduct which reflects this.

The coming together of subtle energy medicine and orthodox medicine can only be for the benefit of patients as the previous polarization has been to their detriment. There is growing pressure from within orthodox medicine, and from complementary practitioners outside, for closer cooperation between doctors, scientists and subtle energy healers. Wherever in the world that Western orthodox medicine is practised, with each new advance in technology, it is becoming possible to scientifically monitor the techniques and effects of spiritual healing. This brings greater understanding and a realization that subtle energy medicine acts according to natural law and that it is not some mysterious placebo effect.

It works because it uses various forms of energy in a highly sophisticated way on the human energy field. Many of these techniques, such as ultrasonics and lasers, are being used in an elementary way by modern medicine. But much remains to be discovered and developed before the two therapies will converge to form the new science of Energy Medicine.

At the first international conference on the 'human energy body' (Le Corps Energetique de l'Homme) in Paris in May 1990, the medical section discussed the notion of the subtle energy body as the interface between body and psyche, able to relay information from one to the other. The energy body played a role in conducting disease-causing information from the psyche to the body, which could therefore be intercepted at this level and be replaced with health-promoting information. They had discovered that specific healing techniques had an effect on the energy body; these included microvibratory energies, electromagnetic energies and spiritual healing. These facts would seem to open the way for the creation of a truly preventative medicine based on cooperation between the relevant therapies.

Scientific trials are being conducted in the UK under the auspices of the CHO. Groups of GPs are conducting similar trials locally, including trials concerned with distant healing. Other countries, such as Japan and the USA, are also conducting trials using sophisticated technology and monitoring methods. These trials include analysis at an atomic and cellular level. As bridges are made between scientists and the various practitioners of subtle energy medicine, a new paradigm of future health care provision is promised.

The health centre of the future is already being created by doctors who have set up pioneering ventures with other complementary therapists. Some are using the 'doorkeeper' system whereby the doctor takes overall responsibility for the patient and recommends a complementary therapy to support his medical treatment . Others are using a system whereby all practitioners are on an equal footing and meet together to work out a pattern for therapy for each individual patient. Spiritual healing has been able to work in both of these settings.

Such clinics will obviously develop according to local needs, but a pattern is already taking shape whereby patients will have a far greater choice of therapy within a totally holistic setting. At some point such provisions will need to become integrated into the public-health system so that its combined expertise will be made available to all who need it.

SELF-HEALING

Another important reason why spiritual healing works is because it cooperates with the body's own healing forces rather than overriding them. The energies of self-healing are stimulated into action as soon as healing is given. In this way we are able to take responsibility for our own health because we control the activities of our own healing energies. When a person is ill or debilitated in any way, he needs outside help to mobilize his own forces, but the outcome will still be determined by his ability or willingness to use healing energy.

People go to see a healer because they need the extra energy input to set their own healing processes in motion or because they do not believe they can channel healing energies themselves. But self-healing is available to all – it simply means putting ourselves into a state of attunement with the Source of healing energies. The simple routine which follows is a way of quickly reaching this state of attunement.

First sit in a comfortable chair with good support for the back. Remove the shoes and allow the feet to rest flat on the ground. Let the arms rest loosely with the hands open, palms up, on the thighs. The elbows should be relaxed and not tense. Close the eyes if preferred or let them rest unfocussed. Allow the breathing to become slow and deep. This is a good posture in which to make ourselves accessible to healing energies.

Now the body needs to relax. Clench the fists tightly then let them slowly unclench. Remember this feeling of unclenching. Let the mind travel down to the left foot and quietly give a mental order to the toes to relax and unclench. Coordinate the gentle, deep breathing with the relaxation

106

technique. Relax and unclench every muscle on the out-breath. Move from the toes over the arch of the foot to the ankle, relaxing and unclenching each muscle and joint. Proceed up the calves, to the knee, then the thighs to the left hip. Now back to the right foot, relaxing and unclenching until the right hip is reached.

Slowly relax the pelvis and groin then move up the front of the body, relaxing and unclenching with the out-breath until the neck is reached. Go back to the buttocks and move up the back of the body, relaxing every muscle in the back. Now move down each arm, from the shoulder to the fingertips, taking care to relax each finger and thumb.

Relax and unclench the neck, up the back of the head, across the top and down over the face, checking that the teeth are unclenched and that the jaw is relaxed. Finally, make a quick scan of the whole body and relax any part which has tightened up again. Any yoga postures and breathing techniques will bring about a similar state of relaxed, tranquil awareness.

The routine is an ideal element in any stress-management programme. If done lying down it will give a lightness and serenity to the body and mind which could lead to sound sleep. In the sitting posture, the ideal state has now been reached for meditation or self-healing. After some practice it can be induced in a few minutes, especially when combined with deep breathing. This means filling the belly first, then the chest, and emptying the belly last.

This meditative state is a state of healing in itself because the body is more aware of the information coming from the higher self (the 'psyche' referred to at the human energy body conference) and there are fewer mental or emotional blocks to this communication. Self-healing simply extends this state to attune to the Source of healing energies. This may be done mentally by prayer, affirmation or whatever statements seem to lift us to this level. Healing may be requested for any condition from which we are suffering or for another who needs help. Remaining as open and relaxed as possible will allow us to experience whatever form the healing might take.

Once we feel it has been completed we should give thanks. This joins the circle of love. Because the whole activity has made our aura more accessible we should gently 'close down' and protect ourselves in the way described in Chapter 3. The process of self-healing could take a matter of minutes either indoors or outdoors. With practice it can even be done while out walking or travelling anywhere. It is an excellent prelude to sleep, last thing at night.

FINDING A HEALER

Few healers advertise though some may be found in local papers and certain journals, some of which are listed towards the end of this chapter. The best procedure is to contact one of the healing organizations which keeps registers of qualified healers and can find one, or perhaps a choice of healers, nearest to a particular locality. A list of these and some healing clinics follows:

Association for Therapeutic
Healers
Flat 5
54–56 Neal Street
Covent Garden
London WC2
Member of CHO

Runnings Park
Croft Bank
West Malvern
Worcs WR14 4BP
Member of CHO

British Alliance of Healing
Associations
26 Highfield Avenue
Herne Bay
Kent CT6 6LM
Member of CHO

Cancer Help Centre
Grove House
Cornwallis Grove
Clifton
Bristol BS8 4PG

Churches Council for Health and
Healing
17 Marylebone Road
London NW1 5LT

Confederation of Healing
Organisations (CHO)
The Red and White House
113 High Street
Berkhamsted
Herts HP4 2DJ

Denton Realisation Healing Centre
Laurel Lane
Queen Camel
Somerset BA22 7NU

Fellowship of Erasmus
The Bungalow, Tollemache Farm
Main Road
Ofton
Ipswich
Suffolk IP8 4RT
Member of CHO

Greater World Christian
Spiritualist Association
3 Conway Street
Fitzrovia
London W1P 5HA

Guild of Spiritual Healers
36 Newmarket
Otley
West Yorks LS21 3AE
Member of CHO

Guild of St Raphael
St Marylebone Parish Church
Marylebone Road
London NW1 5LT

Harry Edwards Spiritual Healing
Sanctuary
Burrows Lea
Shere
Guildford
Surrey GU5 9QG

Healing Centre
91 Fortress Road
London NW5 1AG

Health and Healing Committee
United Reform Church
86 Tavistock Place
London WC1H 9RT
Healing with URC

Hoxton Health Group
St Leonard's Hospital
Nuttall Street
London N1

Jewish Association of Spiritual
Healers
10 Wollaton Road
Ferndown
Dorset

Marylebone Health Centre
Marylebone Road
London NW1

National Federation of Spiritual
Healers
Old Manor Farm Studio
Church Street
Sunbury-on-Thames
Middx TW16 6RG
Member of CHO

Nature Cure Clinic
15 Oldbury Place
London W1

Raphael Clinic
211 Sumatra Road
London NW6 1PF

Spiritual Venturers Association
72 Pasture Road
Goole
North Humberside

Spiritualist Association of Great
Britain
33 Belgrave Square
London Sw1X 8QL
Member of CHO

Spiritualists' National Union
Redwoods
Stansted Hall
Stansted Mountfitchet
Essex CM 24 8UD
Member of CHO

Sufi Healing Order of Great Britain
10 Beauchamp Avenue
Leamington Spa
Warwicks CU32 5TA

White Eagle Lodge
New Lands, Brewells Lane
Rake
Liss
Hants GU33 7HY
Member of CHO

Women's Health Information
Centre
52–54 Featherstone Street
London EC1 8RT

World Federation of Healing
10 Gallards Close
London Road
Southborough
Kent TN4 0N8

Australia

Australian Spiritual Healers
Association
PO Box 4073
Eight Mile Plains
Queensland 4113
Affiliated to the NFSH, UK

Cronus Centre of Australia
MacGregor Hall
Corner of Childers Street
and Barry Drive
Canberra City

CS Church Inc.
123 Caledonian Avenue
Maylands
Western Australia

SNU Centre of Western Australia
579 Murray Street
Perth 6005
Western Australia

Spiritual Mission of St Mary Inc.
9 Torrens Street
Torrensville 5031
South Australia

Canada

National Federation of Spiritual
Healers (Canada)
c/o Mrs Hodgson
TH 64/331
Military Trail
West Hill
Scarborough
Ontario M1E 4E3
Affiliated to the NFSH, UK

Spiritual Sanctuary of Universal
Truth
7220 Miller Road
Richmond
British Columbia V7B 1L4

New Zealand

Auckland Spiritualist Alliance
120 Carlton Grove Road
PO Box 9477
Newmarket
Auckland 1

New Zealand Federation of
Spiritual Healers Inc.
PO Box 9502
Newmarket
Auckland 1
Affiliated to the NFSH, UK.

South Africa

Church of Springs
PO Box 764
Springs 1560
Transvaal

110

CS Church
PO Box 198
Benoni 1500
Transvaal

Psychic Centre
PO Box 12234
Centrahil 6006
Cape Province

USA

The Adobe of the Message
Box 1030D
Shaker Road
New Lebanon
NY 12125

Association for Research and
Enlightenment (ARE)
PO Box 595
Virginia Beach
VA 23451

TRAINING

The following organizations run training programmes on various aspects of healing. It is sensible to study a range of material to see which is most relevant and compatible to yourself.

Courses should be regarded as a means of developing individual healing ability. No course of training will create a healer but it can release and develop healing potential. The best courses are not prescriptive and are run by facilitators who are keen to adapt training to individual needs, recognizing that the ultimate authority is our higher self.

Jack and Jan Angelo
1 Lake Villas
Cwmtillery,
Gwent
N13 1LU

Association for Therapeutic
Healers (see p. 108)

College of Healing
Runnings Park
Croft Bank
West Malvern
Worcs WR14 4DU
Holds regular courses

College of Psychic Studies
The College
16 Queensbury Place
London SW7 2EB
Runs development courses

College of Psychotherapeutics
White Lodge
Stockland Green Road
Speldhurst
Tunbridge Wells
Kent TN3 0TT

Guild of Spiritualist Healers
3 Mayberry Gardens
Hawthorn Lea
Sandyhills
Glasgow G32 0EW

Institute for Advanced Health
Research
51 The Park
Yeovil
Somerset BA20 1DF

National Federation of Spiritual
Healers (see p. 109)

Prometheus School of Healing
152 Penistone Road
Huddersfield
West Yorks

Spiritualist Association
of Great Britain (see p. 109)
Tuition and development
courses

White Eagle Lodge (see p. 110)
Founded by famous medium
Grace Cooke and husband
Ivan,
the Lodge has a worldwide
following

USEFUL ADDRESSES

There are many organizations who are interested in, or encompass, spiritual healing in some way. They cover a wide range of psychic subjects, healing and associated therapies.

Anthroposophical Society in Great
Britain
Rudolf Steiner House
35 Park Road
London NW1 6XT

Association for Palliative Medicine
Royal South Hants Hospital
Brinton's Terrace
Southampton SO2 oAJ
Recognized as a new specialty,
designated Palliative Medicine
(orthodox medicine working with
complementary therapies) by the
Department of Health in 1989

Association for the Scientific Study
of Anomalous Phenomena
c/o Dr Hugh Pincott
St Adhelm's
20 Paul Street
Frome
Somerset BA1 1DX

British Complementary Medicine
Association
39 Prestbury Rd
Cheltenham
Glos
GL52 2P7

British Holistic Medical
Association
179 Gloucester Place
London NW1 6DX

112

Institute for Complementary
Medicine
PO Box 194
London
SE16 1QZ

Maperton Trust
Wincanton
Somerset BA9 8EH
*Charity concerned with spiritual
education*

Michaelmas Trust
10 Irene Road
London SW6 4AL
*Charity concerned with spiritual
education and NDE research*

*Natural Health Network
1 Caxton House
Caxton Lane
Limpsfield
Chart
Surrey RH8 0TD*

USA

American Society of
Alternative Therapists
PO Box 703
Rockport
MA 01966

Foundation for Research on
the Nature of Mind
Box 6847
Durham
NC 27708
*Referrral directory of therapists and
mental-health professionals*

*Healing Light Center
204 E Wilson
Glendale
California 91206*

RESEARCH

The following bodies carry out research into spiritual healing
and specific conditions

Centre for Complementary Health
Studies
University of Exeter
Streatham Court
Rennes Drive
Exeter EX4 4PU

Confederation of Healing
Organisations (see p. 108)

Healing Research Trust
21 Portland Place
London W1N 3AF

Holistic AIDS Research Trust
BM HART
London WC1N 3XX

Research Council for
Complementary Medicine
5th Floor
60 Great Ormond Street
London WC1 3HR

Society for Psychical Research
1 Adam and Eve Mews
London W8 6UG

JOURNALS CARRYING ARTICLES ON SPIRITUAL HEALING

Caduceus
38 Russell Terrace
Leamington Spa
Warwicks CV31 1HE

The Christian Parapsychologist
The Priory
44 High Street
New Romney
Kent TN28 8BZ

Complementary Medical Research
11 New Fetter Lane
London EC4P 4EE
Journal of the Research Council for Complementary Medicine

Fountain International
PO Box 52
Torquay TQ2 8PE

Healing Review
Old Manor Farm Studio
Church Street
Sunbury-on-Thames
Middx TW16 6RG
Journal of the NFSH

Holistic Health
179 Gloucester Place
London NW1 6DX
Newsletter of the BHMA

Holistic Medicine
Baffins Lane
Chichester
Sussex PO19 1UD
Official journal of the BHMA

Journal of Alternative and Complementary Medicine
Mariner House
53a High Street
Bagshot
Surrey GU19 5AH

Kindred Spirit
Foxhole
Dartington
Totnes
Devon TQ9 6EB
Holistic health and environment

Link Up
51 Northwick Business Park
Blockley
Glos GL56 9RF
Holistic health and spiritual matters

Positive Health
51 Queen Square
Bristol
BS1 4LJ

USA

Venture Inward
ARE
PO Box 595
Virginia Beach
VA 23451
Journal of the Association for Research & Enlightenment

Subtle Energies and Energy Medicine
International Society for the Study of Subtle Energies and Energy Medicine
356 Golden Circle
Golden, CO 80403

TAPES ON SPIRITUAL HEALING

Matthew Manning Tapes
39 Abbeygate Street
Bury St Edmunds
Suffolk IP33 1LW

National Federation of Spiritual
Healers (see p. 109)

White Eagle Lodge (see p. 110)

TO CONTACT THE AUTHOR

For further information and/or
advice please contact:
Jack Angelo
Heddfan
1 Lake Villas
Cwmtillery
Gwent NP3 1LU
Wales, UK

Notes and References

1. See Fritjof Capra, *The Turning Point*.
2. 'Spirit helpers'. From the earl. days of healing when levels outside the physical were collectively known as 'spirit', 'the world of spirit' or 'in spirit'.
3. There are many accounts of psychic surgery; see, for example, Philippa Pullar, *Psychic Surgery – Myth or Magic* and Allegra Taylor, *I Fly Out with Bright Feathers*.
4. See Cynthia Pike Ouellette, *Handling Children's Psychic Experiences*.
5. See Findhorn Community, *The Findhorn Garden*.
6. Featured in the ITV film, *The Power of Healing: Apply Within* (May 1990).
7. See, for example, Dennis Barrett's healing of place in *The Healing Spirit* (chapter 4) by Jack Angelo.
8. See, for example, Ian Stevenson, *Children Who Remember Past Lives: A Question of Reincarnation*.

Further Reading

Adamenko, Victor. 'Kirlian Photography', *Caduceus*, Autumn/Winter 1990/91.

Angelo, Jack. *The Healing Spirit*, Rider, London, 1990

Brennan, Barbara Ann. *Hands of Light*, Bantam, New York, 1988.

Butler, W.E. *How to Read the Aura*, Weiser, New York, 1971.

Capra, Fritjof. *The Turning Point*, Fontana, London 1982; Simon & Schuster, New York.
> *The Tao of Physics*, Fontana, London, 1983; Shambhala, USA 1975.

Edwards, Harry. *Psychic Healing*, Spiritualist Press, London, 1946. *A Guide to the Understanding and Practice of Spiritual Healing*, The Healer Publishing Company, Guildford, 1974.

Elliott, Rev. G. Maurice. *The Bible as Psychic History*, Rider, London, 1959.

Findhorn Community. *The Findhorn Garden*, Findhorn Press, Findhorn, 1988.

Hawking, Stephen W. *A Brief History of Time*, Bantam, London, 1988.

Hay, Louise. *Heal Your Body*, Hay House, Santa Monica, 1984.

Herzberg, Eileen. *Spiritual Healing*, Thorsons, Wellingborough, 1988.

Hodges, David & Tony Scofield. 'Science and Spiritual Healing', *Healing Review*, No. 38, Winter 1989.

Horstmann, Lorna. *A Handbook of Healing*, NFSH, Sunbury, 1982.

Kilner, Walter J. *The Human Aura*, Weiser, New York, 1981.

Kübler-Ross, Elisabeth. *On Death and Dying*, Macmillan, London, 1970; New York, 1969.

Leadbeater, C.W. *The Chakras*, Theosophical Publishing House, Wheaton (USA), 1985.

Ouellette, Cynthia Pike. 'Handling Children's Psychic Experiences', *Venture Inward*, Virginia, USA, Sept./Oct. 1990.

Powell, A.E. *The Etheric Double*, Theosophical Publishing House, London, 1973.

Pullar, Philippa. 'Psychic Surgery – Myth or Magic?', *Journal of Alternative & Complementary Medicine*, Bagshot, July 1990.

Schwartz, Jack. *Human Energy Systems*, Dutton, New York, 1980.

Shine, Betty. *Mind to Mind*, Corgi, London, 1990.

Stevenson, Ian. *Children Who Remember Past Lives: A Question of Reincarnation*, University Press of Virginia, USA, 1987.

Storm, Stella (ed.) *Philosophy of Silver Birch*, Psychic Press, London, 1969.

Taylor, Allegra. *I Fly out with Bright Feathers*, Fontana, London, 1987.

TenDam, Hans. *Exploring Reincarnation*, Arkana, London, 1989.

White, Ruth & Mary Swainson. *The Healing Spectrum*, Spearman, London, 1979.

Glossary

Absent healing:— spiritual healing performed at a distance from the patient (in the patient's absence).

Aura:— the emanation of the human spirit and various energy bodies which is seen to surround the physical body; the HEF.

Avatar:— a manifestation of the deity or Source of all energy; Sanskrit, *avatara*.

Bio-energy:— energy associated particularly with organic life.

Blockage:— an accumulation of non-flowing energy causing an obstruction in a human energy system. A blockage may lead to ill health or disease.

Chakra:— an *etheric* structure designed to allow the flow of subtle energies in and out of the HEF; an energy centre; Sanskrit, *chakram*.

Channel:— a medium for the transmission of healing energies and other high-frequency energies, a person who is such a medium; verb: to act as such a medium or instrument.

Clairvoyant:— a person who can perceive or 'see' high frequency energy; Verb: to be clairvoyant is to have a well-developed HSP.

Contact healing:— spiritual healing by the laying of hands upon a patient.

Corona discharge:— the discharge of energy from objects, particularly living things; seen in Kirlian photography as a corona or ring of light.

Distant healing:— *see* absent healing.

Energy Medicine:— developing branch of medicine whereby treatment is largely by application of controlled energies, such as ultrasonics. Energy medicine has always been an important aspect of spiritual healing.

Etheric:— the level of existence next to the physical in which energy vibrates at a higher frequency; known as one of the subtle levels.

Guide:— an entity in spirit form acting as a teacher to an individual or group.

HEF:— the human energy field; *see* aura.

Helper:— an entity in spirit form capable of helping a healer in a range of activities, including surgical.

Higher self:— the spirit aspect of a human being with direct access to, and contact with, the divine Source.

Holistic:— in therapy applied to the whole person rather than a specific part or condition.

HSP:— High sense perception; the natural human ability to sense high frequency vibrations as energy patterns which are perceived in the brain as 'seeing', 'hearing', 'feeling', etc.

Incarnation:— birth on the Earth (physical) plane; the taking on of a physical body as a vehicle for spirit to inhabit.

Level:— a plane of existence where matter vibrates at a certain frequency according to the level; a stage of evolution.

Life force:— the vital energy emanating from the Source which is essential to life.

Medium:— a person with developed HSP, especially one who can sense the presence of entities who no longer have physical bodies; a channel.

NDE:— near death experience; the experience of passing over (death) which can be recalled after resuscitation.

New Age:— the Age of Aquarius. The planetary age recently dawned which will see a great advance in human and planetary evolution.

Out-of-body:— the experience of travelling in the etheric body (being out of the physical body) in which a person is not controlled by physical limitations.

Placebo:— a substance which is medically inactive; substitute for an actual medication which may still act psychologically to produce a medical effect.

Psychic:— psychic senses are those used in HSP; also those based in certain energy centres (chakras) to produce psychic activity; one with psychic abilities is able to control these particular energies, for example, a medium, clairvoyant or healer.

Psychic surgery:— erroneous term for surgical work carried out at a subtle level during certain spiritual healings.

Reincarnation:— being born more than once on the Earth plane; the theory which proposes this process as a natural part of human life and evolution because all life's lessons cannot be learned in one incarnation; not to be confused with the Buddhist doctrine of Karma (Sanskrit, the law of cause and effect) which suggests the possibility of returning as an animal.

Source:— the source of all energy; the law, the power that is; in religious terms – God, the Creator.

Spirit:— a divine spark sent out from the Source on a journey of evolution; all life is spirit; the true aspect of a human being. We are spirits with a body, not bodies with a spirit. Spirits choose various vehicles (bodies) in order to travel on the various levels of existence.

Spiritual:— when referring to healing, using energy emanating from the Source; spiritual activity inclines towards the Source, rather than the limited ego self, to bring about harmony.

Subtle:— of a higher frequency than the physical level, as a 'subtle' body or 'subtle' energy.

UEF:— the universal energy field, the cosmos; electromagnetic field of the universe which contains all energy patterns and transactions.

Index

Absent healing *see* Distant healing
AIDS and healing 13, 18, 93
Animals and healing 13, 39
Attunement 19, 70, 71, 106
Aura 36, 38, 43–6, 55–8, 60, 81, 84

Babies 64, 90
Bach, Dr Edward 77
Baranowski, Dr Frank 57
Barrett, Dennis 71, 117
  Sir William 10, 11
Bereavement and healing 100–102
Bio-energy 44, 119
Black magic 83
Blockage, energy 24, 28, 31, 38, 51, 61, 80, 96, 119
Blocks to healing 25, 54, 58
BMA 13

Cancer Act 10
Cancer and healing 18, 35, 97, 105
Capra, Fritjof 11
Cause and effect, law of 83, 120
Chakra 48–9, 52–4, 80, 119
  Basal 49, 56
  Brow 49, 56
  Crown 49, 50–1, 56
  Heart 24, 28, 31, 49, 50–3, 56, 70, 93, 101–2
  Root 49
  Sacral 49, 51, 56, 68
  Solar plexus 28, 49, 50–1, 56, 59, 70, 80–1, 101
  Splenic 49, 50
  Throat 24, 28, 49, 50–1, 56, 101–2
Channel 63, 83, 88, 106, 119–120
Child healers 64
Children 38–9, 65, 89
  and healing 13, 27, 29, 38–9, 90
CHO (Confederation of Healing Organizations) 13, 66, 104, 109
Church 7, 8, 10
  of Christ Scientist 9
Clairaudience 7, 37
Clairvoyance 7, 37, 45–6, 56–7, 92, 97, 119
Clearing negative energies 55, 70, 82–3
Closing chakras 53–6, 108

Code of Conduct 13, 67
Colour 34, 38–9, 56–7, 77–82
Contact healing 119
Control 12, 26–8, 58
Cornford, Lily 79
Corona discharge 44–5, 119
Counselling 19, 20, 26, 28, 32, 51, 85

Death 96–101
Depression 26, 60, 77, 94
Destiny 26, 90
Distant healing 29, 30, 74–5, 91, 100, 119
Distressed spirits 85–6
Dreams 15, 30, 89, 99

Eddy, Mary Baker 9
Edwards, Harry 5, 6, 10, 75
Ego 52, 120
Emotions 4, 28, 31, 81
Energy, Bio- 44, 119
  blueprint 46
  body 105
  centres *see* Chakra
  medicine 41, 119
  negative 50, 55, 59, 60, 82–5
  system 28, 38
  vitality 47, 50, 53, 82
Environment and healing 75
Essenes 6, 7
Etheric 42, 46, 48, 61, 96, 98, 119
Evolution 4, 71, 76, 92–3, 103, 120
Exorcism 83–4

Faith healing 15
Family Practitioner
  Committees 104
Feedback 15, 74
Finding a healer 108
Force field 20
Forgiveness 24, 28

General Medical Council 6, 13
Grief 100–1
Guardian angel 83
Guides, spirit 20, 66, 119

Hands 1, 2, 14, 42, 45, 69, 74
Haviland, Denis 104

Healers, personal qualities of 58, 63, 65, 69
  Registered 12, 66
Healing
  and confidentiality 13–14, 71
  centre/clinic 12, 101, 104–5
  definition of 1, 5, 16, 17, 22, 40–41, 62
  demonstrations 12, 68
  development of 10
  entities 20, 33–4, 75
  groups 67, 86
  guides 20, 66
  in biblical times 6
  operations 33–5
  session 13–14
  triangle 17, 18, 71, 74, 86
HEF (Human energy field) 38, 42–3, 55–6,
  58, 60, 62, 68, 80, 105, 119
High sense perception (HSP) 7, 37, 39,
  42–5, 50, 56, 78, 97, 119–120
Higher self 3, 4, 23, 52, 64, 67, 115, 119
Hospice 15, 97–9
Hospital 15, 23, 29, 95

Ill health 6, 22–3, 32, 58, 95
  causes of 5
  understanding 22
Illness as a cry for help 29
Incarnation 66, 88, 120
Incurable state 23–4, 40
India 47, 57, 61, 66, 76, 89

Jesus 7

Kahuna 1, 66
Karma 120
Kirlian, photography 44–6, 57, 119
Kübler-Ross, Elisabeth 93, 97

Levels of existence 3, 4, 42, 120
  of healing 19
Life force 47, 53, 96, 120
Love 21, 41, 51–2, 71, 93, 96, 102–3

Maclean, Dorothy 76
Mechanistic world-view 8, 11
Meditation 31, 71, 107
Medium 127
Mental healing 75
  illness 35
Mind 4, 28, 31
Motoyama, Dr Hiroshi 70

National Federation of Spiritual Healers
  (NFSH) 12, 67, 104, 109, 112
Nature spirits 76
Natural Law 83
NDE (Near Death Experience) 97, 99, 120
New Age 64, 92, 105, 120
NHS 105

Old age 95–6
Opening chakras 52
Ouija boards 83
Out-of-body 34, 98, 120

Pain 72–3
Pasricha Dr Satwant 89
Plants 76–8
Prana 47
Pranayama 47
Prayer 30, 75, 107
Pregnancy 91
Previous lives 88–9
Psychic 120
  abilities 9, 35, 92, 94
  energy 50
  experiences 36
  surgery 33–5

Readiness 23, 25
Reincarnation 88–9, 120
Relaxation 14, 16, 106

Sai Baba 57
Satanism 83
Scanning the body 14, 25, 58
Seances 83
Self-healing 106–8
Sensitivity 64–5, 69
Silver 55, 57, 79
Source 17, 52, 67, 83, 120
Spectrum 42, 56, 79
Spirit 3–5, 39–41, 73, 85–90, 96, 120
  guides 20, 66
  helpers 20, 64, 119
  surgery, 33–5
  world, 9
Spiritual 3, 8, 11, 15, 18, 50, 73, 92
Spiritualism 10
Stress elimination 37, 60, 107
Subconscious 4, 71, 89
Subtle 19, 28, 66, 96, 119–120
Suicide 86
Synchronicity 27

Teachers 38–9, 86, 92
Terminal illness 40, 95, 97–9
Therapeutae 7
Third eye 50
Thoughts 16, 31, 59–61, 85, 100
Training 21, 65–8, 71, 114

Unfinished business 24, 95
Universal energy field (UEF) 3, 20, 41, 47,
  84, 120

Witch 7–8

Yodko-Narkevitch, Yakub 44
Yoga 47, 107